TURNING
—THE—
TIDE

TURNING
—THE—
TIDE

Neuroscience, Spirituality and My Path
Toward Emotional Health

Sylvia Bartley PhD

BALBOA.
PRESS

A DIVISION OF HAY HOUSE

Balboa Press books may be ordered through booksellers or by contacting:

Balboa Press
A Division of Hay House
1663 Liberty Drive
Bloomington, IN 47403
www.balboapress.com
1 (877) 407-4847

Print information available on the last page.

ISBN: 978-1-5043-7798-0 (sc)
ISBN: 978-1-5043-7800-0 (hc)
ISBN: 978-1-5043-7799-7 (e)

Library of Congress Control Number: 2017904908

Balboa Press rev. date: 03/29/2017

DEDICATION

To my baby brother Anthony

June 14th 1970 – October 10th 1971

CONTENTS

FOREWORD

It is often said that our character is defined by what we do when we think no one is looking. Sylvia Bartley is one of those rare individuals who is the true embodiment of this axiom. As individuals, it is often our tendency to characterize others based on our observations of their destination rather than our understanding the journey to that destination. It is easy to assume that someone as accomplished as Dr. Bartley has a picture perfect life–beautiful children, a successful corporate career, and the respect and admiration of her community. What someone on the outside looking in may not appreciate, however, is that she was on the receiving end of an early childhood characterized by unimaginable personal heartbreak compounded by social messaging that threatened to crush any hopes of accomplishing her dreams. *Turning the Tide* is Dr. Bartley's personal account of her journey from enduring emotional and near-devastating depression to thriving to a place of wholeness.

As a psychiatrist with a deep interest in the interplay between environmental influences and one's experience of health, *Turning the Tide* speaks to my heart. Depression is often tiptoed around or spoken about only in hushed tones for fear of being considered weak or defective if one were to acknowledge being affected by signs or symptoms of emotional distress. By sharing her experience and understanding of neuroscience Dr. Bartley encourages us to do the opposite; to break the stigma, pay attention to our emotional health and manage it to the best of our abilities with mindful practices. As a neuroscientist, researcher, and spiritual practitioner, Dr. Bartley is in a unique position to understand the intersection between neuroscience and spirituality. This book brilliantly illustrates how these seemingly disparate fields converge in a powerful way. It is this convergence that has allowed Dr. Bartley to transcend adversity and discover the courage to live her truth as not just a physical body but as embodied consciousness. *Turning the Tide* also supports my belief that our genes do not determine our destiny. Lifestyle and environmental influences can dramatically alter the expression of our genes. As a result, our "dis-ease" does not define us but merely serves as a catalyst for further exploration of what our bodies may be trying to communicate via physical and emotional distress. If you have ever struggled with reconciling your rational understanding of the physical nature of the universe with your innate understanding of the nature of spirit, prepare to be delighted.

I first met Dr. Bartley while serving as a presenter at an annual leadership retreat for the Josie R. Johnson Fellowship Program—a program that seeks to identify and nurture future community leaders. I had been invited to speak to the Fellows at a leadership retreat on emotional trauma. Dr. Bartley took the podium shortly after my presentation and effortlessly captivated the room. She is a tall, elegant woman with a deep, rich voice and larger-than-life presence. When Dr. Bartley spoke, people took notice. As co-chair of the Board of Directors for the Minneapolis African American Leadership Forum, she is known as someone who regularly rubs shoulders with the "who's who" of the Minneapolis philanthropic, corporate, and political elite. As the younger generation would say, "she's kind of a big deal." In spite of her many accomplishments, the thing that most stood out about her was not her social status or innumerable achievements, but her humble nature and truly beautiful spirit. I consider myself blessed to have been fortunate enough to forge a friendship with one of the most genuinely kind human beings that I have ever had the pleasure of knowing.

Yours in spirit,

—Reba Peoples

Psychiatrist, M.D.

To a scientist, viewing the world and life in the strictest sense means that most matters will be pretty "textbook." Relationships, power struggles, violence, joy, sadness, and health can all be demystified to basic principles in biological or physical science or those under study. Where do faith, spirit, fate, or religion fit in, or how do they interface with science? When I was in high school one of my classrooms had a small sign with the famous 1954 quote from Albert Einstein: "Science without religion is lame, religion without science is blind." This notion brought me some comfort that both science and our spiritual faith can explain and account for our personal percepts. We all likely fit along some continuum of what balance best creates our sense of purpose or meaning and perhaps we each journey to find our personal equilibrium.

Now, years later, I am a neuroscientist, professor, father, and husband, and similar to Dr. Sylvia Bartley have seen medical science do wondrous things for those in need. And yet we are still mystified by many wondrous things that can't be explained or whether our brain and soul are separate or one and the same. New technologies to study the brain have opened new windows to this query and have spurred new hot topics. The power of our "minds over matter" can create profound neurochemical responses to account for the placebo effect revealing that there is a pharmacy in our own brains ready to remedy our aliments or similarly how our moods can alter our immune health. Our body is far more sophisticated than our conscious minds can grasp, yet we can unleash powerful examples when our faith is put to the test.

In this remarkable journey of spirituality and science, Dr. Sylvia Bartley shares her many experiences that unite her inner faith with her objective training and career as a neuroscientist. Sylvia's life has been unique and personal yet her path to transcendence and finding peace and emotional health will be relevant to all who seek such balance. Battling the remnants of racism and gender bias in a seemingly inclusive world, enduring the commitments of earning her PhD, standing up to the insensitive, caring for her family, and confronting personal demons builds the fabric of this fascinating autobiography. Sylvia is a dear friend and former colleague of many years and our paths have crossed many times on topics of how advances in medicine are for healing the individual as well as the patient. I invite you to share in her experiences to help foster enlightenment out of your life travels.

Gregory F. Molnar, PhD

Associate Professor—Department of Neurology at the University of Minnesota School of Medicine

"I write for those women who do not speak, for those who do not have a voice because they were so terrified, because we are taught to respect fear more than ourselves. We've been taught that silence would save us, but it won't." –Audre Lorde

Audre Lorde described what so many of us have felt. We've all been there. A dark, closed and yet familiar place that we turn to when the pressures of work, family, or relationships threaten to overwhelm us. Here, we are invisible when life gets to be too much. We don't want to be here but it is the place that we can count on. It seeks us out. It will not disappoint us. It is familiar. And it keeps us silent. Women, and black women in particular, have been taught to keep our feelings of sadness, fear, and pain to ourselves. We are told, "be strong, that this, too, will pass." It does pass but not without taking a toll on our health in the process. Audre Lorde captures black women's long and arduous history of marginalization and invisibility that has forced us to question our abilities, satisfy others first, do it all and bear it all, in silence.

In our community, we do not generally speak openly about emotional health or mental illness. We do not say depression, schizophrenia, or bipolar. We say, "Tamara's down today" or "Kim's not herself" or "I've got the blues." We also tend not seek professional help for mental illness and when we do, we are often underdiagnosed or completely misdiagnosed within the mental health system. And black women who do seek therapy will often struggle with insurance limitations or the lack of culturally sensitive mental-health professionals who can meet our unique needs. All of this is understandable. The stress of racism, sexism, and classism has created an environment where we do not trust the seemingly good intentions of healthcare providers. Black women are at increased risk for mental-health problems and psychological distress. In our community, to be depressed is to be weak. So, to handle these stressors, we turn to our faith. We try to "pray the pain away."

At the Black Women's Health Imperative, we see how stress and pain are expressed in women's health every day. Thirty-four years ago, we began as a self-care organization because there was a need for safe spaces for black women to talk about their pain, that to be silent about something so profound was to deny our very humanity. Research has shown that black women have elevated levels of the stress hormone cortisol in our bloodstreams. This triggers our inflammatory response and raises our risk for diabetes, hypertension, cancer, and other chronic conditions. It also increases our allostatic load, the wear and tear on our bodies. The effect of this wear and tear is that by the time we're sixty, our bodies have aged five to seven years faster than those of our white counterparts.

While we may pride ourselves on being strong, the inconvenient truth is that we can no longer take a passive approach to meeting our mental-health needs. Thankfully, one woman had the courage to share her deeply personal experience to help us understand that we can take control of our mental health, that we are not victims and that science and spirituality combined are powerful force for healing.

In this book, *Turning the Tide*, Sylvia Bartley grants us an unvarnished view of her journey through depression, coping, vulnerability and, ultimately, awareness as she discovers that science and spirituality are, in fact, mutually reinforcing properties of emotional well-being. In many faith traditions, we are taught that science and spirituality are incongruent. One cannot be both a scientist and a woman of faith. That notion is disrupted here as we are shown how spirituality makes us healthier and how neuroscience underpins our modern spiritual concepts.

In the first chapter, "The Personal," we are shown how Sylvia's unusual experiences have contributed to her feelings of isolation and bold exploration. From growing up black in London, to surviving open heart surgery and not speaking for an entire year, to pursuing a PhD in neurophysiology as a mother of young children, Sylvia describes the self-doubt, humiliations, and fears that threatened to drag her to unrecoverable depths. Despite her brilliance and successes, she still questioned and denied her accomplishments as if somehow they had been accidental. What she would discover in Paris shook her to the very core and nearly ended her life.

The following chapters, "The Spiritual" and "The Scientific," reveal the dark dream that haunts Sylvia, the evil she believes is hers to be a revelation. It put her on an incredible and grueling path to spiritual discovery and opened her mind to the possibility that science can lead to awakening. Research shows that meditation and spiritual practice can actually create new neural pathways in the brain that, in turn, make us more aware and more connected to our emotions and the ability to heal. Our brain chemistry, like our emotional state, is not fixed. We all have ANTS–automatic negative thoughts that result in FEAR–false evidence appearing real. In this book, one woman's bravery shows us that we can peel back the layers of these thoughts to reveal truth of who we are. And that we can love who we see.

In the final chapter, "The Convergence," the coping strategies we've all tried, denying our emotions, submerging ourselves in work, being the perfect parent, over-eating and many others are laid bare. Sylvia explains through her discovery that the physical expression of health depends on our spiritual awareness. Our souls require "recognition and constant nurturing." Sylvia notes, "many who practice meditation believe the primary outcome is inner peace, tranquility, and sometimes transcendence– being more open to spiritual beliefs and practices." Her journey will show that this is just the beginning, not the end. Understanding neuroscience has expanded her awareness beyond this realm to improving her physical health as well.

Most survivors of serious illnesses will talk of how their lives have been positively changed by their experience. Sylvia describes her depression as a gift. She says, "It's the force in my life that pushes me to finally take care of myself, to seek answers in both spirituality and scientific academia, and to use those answers to affect others on their own paths."

We at the Black Women's Health Imperative will take the lessons so generously shared by Sylvia Bartley to the millions of women we reach each year. This book deepens our understanding of the unique struggles Black women experience by illuminating the unspoken realities of pain and suffering that we are conditioned to ignore. She has given voice to our lived experiences, she has created the safe space in which we can talk about our pain and she has given us tools we can use every day to heal. This book is indeed a gift to black women and to all women who have struggled to find peace, and who are on a path to achieve emotional well-being. Sylvia had the courage to break her silence—we will not let her voice go unheard.

Linda Goler Blount

President & CEO, Black Women's Health Imperative

GRATITUDES

From my heart, I'm grateful to all who entered my life as a nurturer, guide, teacher, supporter, cheerleader, protector, counselor, or friend. Those who have helped me evolve along my continual quest for enlightenment, internal peace, and happiness. Without my village I would not be possible. My village has encouraged me to stay on my path, it has carried me through the most difficult times, comforted me when I felt forsaken, and gave me hope when I felt like giving up. My village is made up of light beings from all different walks of life.

To my beloved mother, whose strength, beauty, brilliance, resilience, creativity, and the sheer power of her spirit will always shine a light in my heart. Our connection is one where words cannot adequately express the gratitude, appreciation, and love we have for each other. I understand why we choose each other and I'm grateful to have been blessed with such an example of fortitude in my life. My mother taught me many valuable life lessons—one being the power of service. By giving unreservedly to her church community, I witnessed firsthand the impact she had on people's lives, helping me to completely understand why service matters. Unconsciously she gave me permission to do the same wherever I lay my hat—the place I call home. It's a lesson I will always appreciate to its full extent.

To my darling children Andrew and Portia, the apple of my eye, my heart and soul—two young adults any parent would be proud to call their own. Core to who we are is the unconditional love we hold for each other. Through thick and thin we always lean into our soul connection, loving and supporting each other along our individual paths to enlightenment. Andrew and Portia have taught me so much about real unconditional love, individualism, the art of reason, and creativity. They've shown me the power of following your heart and doing what makes you happy, how to value one's self and believe in one's abilities to do whatever it is we choose to do. They've shown me what courage looks like to stand in your truth, and more importantly they've shown me what it looks like to be free. For these and the many other gifts my children have brought into my life I'm eternally grateful. I wrote this book with both of them in mind, in the hope it will inspire them to strive to be the best person they can be in this lifetime. I love them both dearly—thank you Andrew and Portia for being such a force in my life.

Sisterhood is a special bond: we know it, we feel it, we embrace it and we need it. I'm grateful to all of my sisters for supporting me along my journey and for encouraging me to write this book. My siblings, Monica, Sandra, and my extended family are key people in my village I'm grateful for. Thank you for being that stoic, reliable support everyone needs in their lives. You bring me joy and for that I will always be grateful. To my sister girls–you know who you are. I'm grateful for your wisdom, fellowship, guidance, and honesty. I'm grateful for the safe spaces and trust we have developed to be ourselves, and for the opportunities to delve into deep conversations that evoke our minds and stir our souls.

To my editors, Shannon Pennefeather Gardner and Erik Hane, You are amazing, thoughtful, and talented editors. Thank you for pouring your heart into my manuscript and giving it the attention required to shape it into a nice story. To Linda, Greg, and Reba, I'm grateful you took the time to read and write a foreword for my book. It's meant the world to me and I appreciate your kind words and thoughtful review.

To my father, it was tough! As the old adage goes everything happens for a reason. I know our relationship propelled me on my path to spiritual awareness. Even today I feel your presence and still see you in my dreams watching over me, trying to connect and make peace. I know your heart is with us and recognize you loved us. I understand— it's time to rest peacefully and put an end to the suffering. We are at peace and I'm grateful for that.

To my God, my energy source, my light, and my protector. To the power greater than us—your love is boundless. I pray every day to remain open to hear and receive you in all your glory. Thank you for protecting and loving me. Thank you dear Lord for never giving up on me, thank you for helping me to see the light.

INTRODUCTION

The waves form far out in the Caribbean Sea, a distant edge of the horizon from where I'm sitting. Everywhere I look, I see life. Birds flying so skillfully overhead, in tandem, blending in to the humid landscape of waves and palm trees that my son watches intently as well. Another huge swell tears toward us, threatening to wash us away, crashing instead into the rocks before us that serve as guardians against the roar of the water. The foamy tide creeps down the beach and back into the sea. My son and I breathe deeply, in tandem just like the gulls.

Sylvia, it is time for the tide to turn. I hear this in myself and it feels as though the rocks are saying it, though I know it is my spiritual guides. *You are protected, and it is time.* Time for what, I wonder at first, but I already know. Time to rise from the emotional despair I am too often mired in, time to beat back the sea of insecurities that plague my spiritual life. It is time, as it so frequently has been in my life, to master my own mind so as to better hear my own spirit. Another wave crashes, another gull cries. Let Montego wash over me, clean like the beach beyond which I see the setting of the watery sun.

Another feeling emerges and consumes my thoughts as the waves continue to make their presence vehemently known. Montego Bay, the same beautiful shores where my ancestors were brought against their will generations ago. What must they have thought arriving at this beautiful place only to begin yet another horrific journey? I can't even imagine the emotional distress they endured without any reprieve. The scene is different now though as the waves pick up speed near the shore, crashing into the rocky peninsula and splashing a mist high in the air—I'm here with my son on a spur-of-the-moment Christmas trip, a chance to get away from it all for at least a little while. My spirit needs this, which means my mind does too.

An increasingly strong relationship is being drawn between spirituality and science, perhaps most specifically spirituality and neuroscience. It's has been an antagonistic relationship that borders on flat-out opposition: spirituality is an outdated tool for understanding our minds, and its answers are gradually and continually supplanted by the findings of modern neuroscience. In short, everything spirituality has to offer may be replaced or justified by scientific understanding of the brain. On the flip side, those who dig in their heels on the side of religion or spirituality often argue that science is far too reductive to be fully used to understand ourselves; we are far more than the sum of our biological parts. From these positions the battle lines get drawn, and crossing from one side to the other means facing profound skepticism from peers in either camp.

All this said, is it any wonder that both science and spirituality present incomplete pictures of our interior selves? The more we understand about the human brain through neuroscience, the clearer it becomes just how little we know. This might be the defining feature of the field (and perhaps all of science): the more territory that gets discovered and charted, the larger the remaining blank spaces in the map present themselves to be. It is a process of learning what we don't know. And as those gaps present themselves, spirituality is happy to jump in and point them out as mysteries that can only be addressed through nonscientific thought. That holds until neuroscience *does* fill in that specific gap, which of course creates new gaps, and the cycle continues. It will continue forever.

This would be fine to treat as just a discussion of ideas if the two fields weren't meeting in one very human and applicable place: our emotional and mental well-being. In an age when we are more concerned and knowledgeable than ever about the effects our emotional health can have on our lives, does it do us any good to wage this endless fight between science and spirituality? It's one thing to have this argument in a lab or a classroom; it's another to tell someone battling depression that we just don't have the answers yet, and that anywhere they turn they will only find incomplete information. When a person is in the throes of depression, or any other neurophysical imbalance what we are increasingly learning are very common, that person does not care so much which side the answers come from. I can say this very confidently; I am a person fighting that fight to achieve and maintain good emotional health

A lot of people might find it strange that I am both a neuroscientist and a spiritual person. In fact, these are the two labels that have worked together to shape my life. My journey to this point has two consistent threads, one of rigorous academic study and another of spiritual exploration. These two things were my foundation as a child and young student and are still my primary focus as an adult. I could hardly afford not to pay attention to them; depression is a constant presence in my life, and so I've had to search for ideas, habits, and solutions practically as a means of survival.

My story is one that takes these two seemingly opposed fields that have defined my life and blending them together in a pursuit of truth and well-being. My spiritual life has evolved drastically throughout my life, and I attribute this to the way I've applied my scientific curiosity and discipline to learning more about spiritual practice. By the same token, my scientific career would not have reached the point it has, if not for my ability to stay spiritually attuned to myself in the midst of rigor and adversity. And this is what I wish to illustrate in this book: neuroscience and spirituality are not opposites, but actually complement one another in a way that can further each field. Furthermore on a human, individual level, the blending of these two modes of thought can have tremendous effects on our emotional health.

That personal level feels essential to this discussion, because too often these ideas get lost in the abstract beyond ourselves. I am a person who has battled depression, and a person who has used both spirituality and a credentialed academic career in neuroscience to do so. Much of this book is my story.

As a girl, I spent my childhood emotionally closed off from others because of a culture that constantly taught me that feelings were meant to be kept to myself. This, I believe, is when my depression took root. I carried it through into adulthood, where my pursuit of a doctorate in neuroscience had me facing my own emotional turmoil at the same time as I experienced some racism, misogyny, and disrespect along my journey. While others see no connection between neuroscience and spirituality, I see no way to separate them. I needed each to help fuel my pursuit of the other, and I need both to this day to help me stay well, achieve my goals, and raise my children. Even on the basis of learning how to find stability and basic happiness while living with depression, mine is a success story, and for that reason alone it's worth sharing with the countless people in this country and others who are struggling too.

Despite constant progress in studies on emotional health, depression (in its many forms) still carries a stigma that threatens to leave far too many of us undiagnosed or misdiagnosed. This is in large part because of a widespread reluctance to come forward and seek help, tied to a general feeling of not knowing whom to turn to, or to which practices. I want my story, and the scientific and spiritual thoughts I layer on top of it, to show that even in the face of brutal depression, spiritual growth and emotional health are possible. The first step, though, is to make ourselves vulnerable, to remove the walls we've placed around our spiritual emotional selves. The first step is revealing who we are—to others, to God, and even just to ourselves.

The act of thinking through and writing this book represents one more instance in my life of exploring that vulnerability. By sharing my experiences and being forced to work through my spiritual beliefs on the page for others, I am opening myself up once again. By outlining my twisting path to well-being, I am reminded of it, because I still need to be. This is because a journey with true depression is never fully over; it involves reflection, thinking, and sharing that constantly challenge us to grow and take care of ourselves. I am still on that journey, regardless of how much progress I've made in thinking through it from both scientific and spiritual perspectives.

While that sounds like never-ending work (which it is), it is also a sacred gift: my depression has forced me to grow and expand myself in ways I never would have without it. This too is a central point of this book. By dealing with depression, we can be made stronger. My life has been a search for answers for dealing with the darker parts of my mind; In doing so I have formed beliefs and spiritual habits that are priceless aids in times of mental turmoil and incredible assets in times of stability and wellbeing. As such, I can incontrovertibly say that my depression has made me better: a better neuroscientist, a more nuanced spiritual thinker, and a person far more attuned with herself than that insular, troubled girl in my past would have imagined.

I have found meaning in my depression, and I believe that meaning exists for others suffering as well. This is the lifelong challenge through which my soul is growing, the process through which I will emerge—and in some ways, already have emerged—as an enlightened person.

This, then, is the task at hand. Here, I will take you through my life, focusing on the moments and experiences most influential in my becoming the scientifically spiritual person I am today. I will discuss the neuroscientific concepts that underpin much of our modern spiritual discussions, and then see how these concepts blend with my spiritual beliefs. Finally, I hope to show you how focusing on spiritual practice is more than just "making things up," as many people believe; these practices can have real neurological effects. Speaking strictly in terms of biology, spirituality can make us emotionally healthier. On the flip side, there's an understanding science can help us focus on our spiritual efforts.

Here is my story. It's one that uses formative personal experience to combine scientific knowledge with spiritual belief, and in that way it's a story that doesn't have to be different from those of other people. It's a story of turning the stigma of depression into strength, by revealing that when it comes to our mental health, spirituality and science aren't the enemies we thought they were.

DEPRESSION

I can't get out of bed even though I desperately try. My head is a dark, remorseful place all but disconnected from a world I now feel I'm looking into from the outside. I need my people, those who understand me and provide the space for me to exist without judgment, an agenda, or expectations. Whatever my lesson is from this lifetime, I am tired of it; I've learned it many times over.

I bury my throbbing head deeper into my pillow. My soul is pleading for salvation, to be taken away from this world into another. I am beyond exhausted. So I pray for forgiveness, for guidance. But the throbbing in my head grows louder and I feel like my brain might erupt. My throat is sore; I struggle to breathe. My heart beats harder; my chest rises sharply. I wheeze and it feels like something is trying to climb out of me.

The feeling of guilt rushes over me, and I surrender to my God. I should be grateful for so many things in my life: my dear children, my mum, my sister, and friends who I know would be distraught if I left them. And so I face the persistent question: what reasons do I have to be unhappy? I feel as though I'm nothing, despite everything I'm proud of, everything I've accomplished. And I feel something worse, that I am the only one who can stop this feeling. I start pleading, begging for forgiveness that despite all that's been given to me—my family, my job, a life that I would never trade—I still feel this way. I plead to be taken home.

Then everything calms down—my heavy breathing ceases, my head stops throbbing, and my heartbeat slows to a steady pace. A sense of peace envelops me. I relax into this renewed clarity. It travels along a dark passage and right there in front of me is my living son's spirit, pure love pouring from his heart in my direction. His love surrounds me, touches me, and comforts me. Our spirits merge and I feel nothing but his sweet, tender love. He heard my cry and came to my aid, my beautiful son. I hang onto this feeling for dear life while I allow my emotions to release—my head and heart start to pound against their confining walls. The throbs reach a deafening crescendo. I struggle to breathe again as I hang onto my loving son's spirit.

Then my mind travels to my daughter. I feel her pain and panic. I enter into her spirit but I can't stay there for long. She is too distressed—I get the message. She loves me, I know that, and she needs me here with her right now. So does my son. A voice: "Now is not the time to give up." These visions prove to be just enough for me to continue.

So I get up, slowly but willingly wiping my tears and putting my feel-good practices into play. I play my uplifting spiritual music: "How Awesome is our God" followed by "Optimistic" and "Rise Up," which I play again and again and again. I fall on my knees, dazed, and I pray for strength and guidance: how, God, am I supposed to put any of this to good use? What now? Why am I here?

The tears keep flowing as I get dressed. I will myself to the gym, plug into my gospel music and work out like crazy, stimulating the endorphins to kick in quickly. This is hard work. The counter-chatter to my negative thoughts is working hard to be heard. I also hear my mum's voice telling me to "get on with it, keep it moving, so I do, but I feel invisible; I'm mindlessly existing, going through the motions of life. I leave the gym with as little energy as when I arrived and I drive home.

I see a large object in the middle of my lane on the freeway. I swerve to avoid it, into what I think is a clear left lane, but it isn't clear; in a split second an SUV is right there, enormous in my mirrors. Before I know what's happened I'm back in my lane and the SUV has sped past me, so close I feel the breeze brush my face even though the windows are rolled up. At that moment of somehow avoiding collision, all my fears release: I realize I am protected. I hear another message very clearly. "You're not going anywhere yet–you have work to do here." I am stunned—and grateful. It shakes me out of myself and jolts me back into existence. My heart is racing so fast and I feel immense appreciation for life–my life.

PART I

THE PERSONAL

For as long as I can remember I have existed more inside my head than outside it. Thinking, wishing, dreaming to be in a different place, somewhere I could feel like I belonged. And with this feeling of displacement naturally comes one of isolation, of sadness; I felt separate from the same people from whom I desperately sought acceptance. Consequently, I withdrew at a very young age so that I simply existed: I did what was expected of me, and little more. I had experiences in my youth, education, and career that deeply hurt my feelings and damaged my self-esteem. In most cases, instead of expressing my reactions, I kept them to myself because of a belief that such things must remain hidden from view. I have a name for this cycle of withdrawal, now: My Depression. And I offer this account of my early life experiences and background to set the tone for the evolution of my thinking about My Depression, spirituality, and the science that supports a spiritual approach to manage My Depression.

Sylvia Bartley PhD

ORIGINS

My mother and father were hardworking people from the Caribbean islands of St. Lucia and Jamaica, respectively. They were part of a mass migration in the 1950s and '60s, after many of the Caribbean people who had assisted Britain during World War II had returned home. As part of the British Empire, many Caribbean people joined the British Royal Air Force (RAF) during the war to make up for the shortage of RAF pilots, returning to the Caribbean after the war. Then, in June 1948 the Empire Windrush boat docked in England with hundreds of people from the Caribbean who sought a new life in Great Britain.

My mother, Rose Elliott, arrived alone in the UK in the 1960s at the tender age of nineteen. Like other black immigrants, my parents often faced hostility and blatant racism from the British. While the British embraced the Caribbean people during the Second World War, they resented them seeking to work and live in Great Britain in the years that followed the conflict. Racism was a new and shocking experience for my mother, who never expected or understood why people treated her badly in a place that had portrayed itself as an ally to the Caribbean people. "No dogs, no blacks, no Irish," read signs my parents often saw in the windows of rental housing accommodations.

My mother met my father, Eric Samuel Headlam, a tall man from Kingston, Jamaica, shortly after her arrival in Great Britain. They married and had three daughters and a son. My parents worked tirelessly to provide for our family. They lived in a challenging rental accommodation before purchasing a home in a predominantly white neighborhood in Croydon Surrey. It was here in this small three-bedroom townhouse where I was raised with my two sisters. I don't have much recollection of my early years, but I do remember sleeping on a single camp bed with Monica and Sandra while my mum slept on an ottoman when we first moved into our new home. I must have been around three years old. I think they were the only pieces of furniture we possessed at the time. My father once showed me his weekly pay slip of five pounds, which was not much money at all. It wasn't easy being black in Great Britain, but through perseverance, resilience, and hard work my father's salary increased sufficiently to run a household and invest in savings. Over the years, our house filled with furniture.

My father worked every day until he retired, at the post office on Blackfriars Bridge in London. I don't know what his role was, but he rarely took time off. Working at night meant he slept for most of the day, which allowed us some time to relax in our home. He was hard on us. I feared him; he rarely gave us any of the obvious indicators of parental love or emotion. Rarely did we get a hug, and I can't remember ever being told I was loved. That word was foreign in our house, spoken instead through action: making sure we were home on time, having high expectations of us, and scolding us for not being where we were supposed to be. We knew our parents cared for us by the sheer force of their attention.

On a few occasions my father would sit down with me and tell me some stories of his early years in England. He loved cricket, and we would watch The Ashes together when he was home. He would jump up for joy when Vive Richards scored yet another six and Clive Lloyd would bat the West Indies to victory. This was back when the West Indies cricket team dominated Great Britain; we felt a real sense of pride in watching their victories together.

That was the pleasant side of my father. But he was also very strict, and often exhibited strange moods that resulted in him being unbearable, berating us for the simplest things like turning on the lights or making the slightest noise. Children were to be seen and not heard in those days, and that was certainly the case in our house.

So in general I never questioned my parents and was obedient most of the time. I remember once lashing out, screaming at my father for his ridiculously strict rules and reprimands, and while it got me nowhere I did feel better afterwards, at least for a short while. But then the guilt of being disrespectful to my father overwhelmed me into apologizing, in order to make peace with myself. This cycle—emotion and guilt and apology—would be one I would become highly familiar with. I had a difficult childhood under my father's rule, and I attribute this as one of the main sources of my negative self-image. He passed away on April 14, 1999, at the age of seventy-four.

That is not the end of my relationship with my father. Almost every week since his death, he has visited me in my dreams. Usually he just watches in the background; sometimes he says something, but most times he does not. He asks questions about new friends, and recently he frantically screamed about wanting to be with his children. His distressed concern for us was a reminder that despite his behavior, he cared for us very deeply.

I believe my father suffered for many years with some type of psychological disorder, maybe some form of depression or a bipolar disorder. I'm not a physician or psychiatrist. This diagnosis may explain his irrational, challenging behavior, and by extension it probably helps explain some of my depression. Seeking help for any kind of emotional disorder wasn't and still isn't a common practice in the UK black community. It manifests in abnormal behavioral issues and is deemed as such, something to be contained and managed within the family. Therefore, most suffer in silence and are typically punished for their illness. It breaks my heart to know that my father walked this painful path in silence. And as he suffered, we all suffered, yet we stayed loyal to him.

My mother devoted herself full time to us, and did her best to make amends for my father's behavior. She worked equally hard around the home. She was and still is very creative. She made the majority of our clothes, which were equal to and most times better than the clothes found in department stores. It was exceptionally useful having tailor-made clothes, especially when we became tall young adults with long limbs. We didn't have the issue of finding clothes to fit us, and it was fun choosing patterns and fabrics with my mum for our new outfits. We would make special trips to Brixton to buy fabrics, Caribbean food, and black hair products. It always felt good to be amongst fellow black people.

The center of my mother's life was her Catholicism. She was always devout, and spent (and still spends) copious hours at the church, lending her skills and volunteering her spare time supporting the church operations, parishioners, and priests.

My father was a Methodist and went to church most Sundays alone while we attended our morning Catholic service at St Mary's Church. To this day, my mother and sister still attend St Mary's Church on a regular basis. This is the church I got married in, and where I baptized my two children. The presence of God was strong in our house and if by any chance we forgot, a large picture of the Sacred Heart of Jesus (a white man with long blond hair, striking blue eyes, and pierced bleeding palms faced outward towards us) was a stark reminder of our faith.

My sisters and I went to a high-performing, strict Catholic school, from infant school (kindergarten), middle school (elementary), and high school. St. Mary's Catholic School was affiliated with the Church we attended, and this is where the Catholic teachings and practices were reinforced to us daily. A generation later, my children attended St.

Mary's as well. Being raised a Catholic provided me with the fundamental principles of my belief in the universe, and in the existence of something greater than us mortal humans. While I never felt connected to the Catholic doctrine, I did feel very connected to my God. During Mass I would tune out from the external world and tune in to my internal world, connecting and enjoying unrestricted conversations with God. I was not aware of practices like meditation back then; I was simply aware of the peace I felt when I managed to connect with myself on a deep, internal level.

It's relatively straightforward to see how someone like me could become deeply introverted, even at a young age. I was being raised in a culture where loving feelings were not generally expressed willingly. At the same time, we were exposed during our formative years to a religion that placed a premium on quiet prayer and strict teaching, delivered to us through a rigorous and challenging religious system. These somewhat common traits of my upbringing are only part of the story. A poignant moment of grief at a young age would also cause me to turn ever more fully inward toward myself.

In 1970 my mother gave birth to my baby brother Anthony. To me, he just appeared in our house in a cot in the corner of my mother's room. I had no idea my mother was expecting a child, which meant my brother's arrival came as a wonderful surprise. I fell in love with him when I saw his small head full of black curly hair sleeping in the cot. I vowed to connect with and be close to him, even at my age of four.

I recall one evening my sisters and I were sitting on the bed in a circle talking and keeping each other distracted, as we believed we were in the house alone. No lights were on in the house. All of a sudden my mother appeared, and from the dark doorway she stood in her voice sounded quiet, weaker than we'd ever heard. "Anthony is gone. He died." Anthony, at fifteen months, had suddenly passed away from pneumonia.

My next memory of this tragic loss was standing in the morgue, holding my mother's hand, and looking into a small coffin where my brother peacefully lay. He was smartly dressed in blue trousers and a white shirt, a blue rosary around his neck. His lips were dry, his eyes shut, and he looked peaceful. I was confused. Death confused me, and from that moment on I feared it. I feared not knowing why he was taken away, or where his spirit went. I could see his body, but I knew I wasn't seeing him. It was too much for me to comprehend and I refused, point blank, to go the funeral. I stayed at home with a neighbor while everyone else went to the funeral.

People came to our house afterwards and the only thing I recall is my mother sitting on a chair in the living room crying. I didn't know what to do or think. I just knew I feared death and never wanted to get this close to it again. I remember weekly visits to his grave in the cemetery after Sunday mass, bringing offerings of flowers and prayers. We would clean up his headstone and spend time in prayer and reflection. It felt okay to be there with him, but it also triggered questions in my mind revolving around the meaning of life or life after death. These were questions to which my religion at the time never gave a satisfactory answer, but I kept asking and searching for answers internally.

Death shocked me. It snatched away a loved one who'd barely started living. This was terrifying. Witnessing or being impacted by the death of someone close was a new experience, a far-off concept reserved for people at the ends of their lives. I was learning that this, it turned out, was true; however, the "end" didn't have to wait until we were ready or reached an old age. We had no power over death, we could not tell it what to do. It made me wonder about life after death, as well as life before we were brought into this world. I became a seeker searching for the answers to my questions.

After much seeking over the years I now have an understanding of the journey of souls. Our souls—my brother's soul—move from one life to another, existing in various forms based on the lessons that need learning by both him and those of us around him. I have learned from him; his time here was not wasted. His spiritual guide has led him elsewhere now, just as mine leads me, and I believe we're both profoundly better and spiritually evolved for having known each other the brief time that we did.

No surprise, then, that I became more introverted during my childhood. My mother told me I refused to speak for a whole year after I had open-heart surgery. Fortunately, the surgeons were considerate enough to open me up from the back. Although they had to work through my ribs during the procedure, I was not left with a big scar down my chest, just a moderate one on the posterior side of my spine. I had what is now called a hole in my heart, the congenital condition patent ductus arteriosus (PDA).

To reiterate, there are many holes in my childhood memory. I don't recall feeling ill or even going to doctors. I do, however, remember lying in a hospital bed being wheeled to the Operating Room (OR). I was excited, because I knew I was going somewhere important, but concerned at the same time. My mother was sitting by herself in a big room, with her head down crying. I waved to her, I called out to her but she was too overcome with grief to wave back or even look up. It was strange, seeing her like this; we were not an emotional family and yet here she was, letting her grief flow freely. Writing this book I discovered my operation was just a few months after my brother passed away. To this day, I cannot imagine what painful emotions my dear mother must have experienced during that time. Her youngest child lost so suddenly to pneumonia, and now her next youngest being wheeled into an OR to undergo a new and risky open-heart procedure. It's no wonder she was suddenly wearing her heart on her sleeve. Where did my mother turn, in her time of distress? Did she look to her faith in God to carry her through? Did she find some untapped reservoir of strength inside herself? I don't know how she did it, and I'm not sure she entirely does either; but she did, and I would learn much later in my life that persevering in moments that felt impossible was a trait she had passed on to me.

Then I was in a strange room with tall men in loose green clothes and green Wellington boots. They stood in a huddle with their hands clutching each other, their fingers crossed in their cream colored gloves. Now I know they were in scrubs, scrubbed up and waiting to start the procedure. Once in a while they would look at me and ask, "Is she asleep yet?" The answer was clearly no, as I was asking for water to drink. I was so thirsty and hot in that room. I had no clothes on, but that did not concern me.

That's all I remember. I don't remember waking up in intensive care, where I spent several days before being transferred to the ward. I do remember helping a nurse by carrying her injection tray while she would give injections to the other children. My mother told me I was in intensive care for a while and in considerable pain for at least a year after the operation. That's one of the reasons I refused to talk. I didn't understand why I had the surgery or why I was in pain. I couldn't lift my left arm for many months. When I came home from the hospital my sisters said I sounded like Mickey Mouse, their teasing becoming one more reason why I didn't speak. The biggest reason was my playmate; my sweet brother was taken away and wasn't coming back. I had turned deeply inward, by now. There was nothing for me outside of myself; it was clear I didn't belong here.

I never spoke about my negative thoughts or depressed moods, because at the time I didn't label them as such. I just knew I was different and focused more internally than most. It was my norm. This approach to my own personhood certainly manifested itself in my school life, where I felt different and hardly spoke to anyone. I was labeled shy, and realize now that I was an unsure person trying to understand my purpose in life. I had a few good friends, and as I got older and came out of my shell a bit I became quite popular. I was a seeker, searching for a place where I felt comfortable.

Entering my teenage years, I became conscious of a major difference between myself and the little world I lived in: the color of my skin. Here was an obvious outward reason why I felt different. All my friends and teachers were white. I was one of two black people in my class, and while my friends liked me for who I was, I became tired of feeling different and realized that I wanted friends who looked like me. So I went out and found them.

One of them came from the class a year or two below me, where there was an emergence of black students. A girl I got to know had brothers in a different, predominantly black school. During the summer holidays I had no plans, so one day I went to her house and hung out with her and her brothers and their friends, most of whom were black-conscious people. This was a bold move for me: I didn't know her well, but still took it upon myself to turn up at her home unexpectedly. They were open to me. I was teased at times, for wearing thick glasses and for being studious. It was nothing I wasn't used to. Through this friendship I entered into the world of black culture, black music, foods, dances. It was new and exciting, and I began to feel comfortable with them.

I made good friends and enjoyed my times with them, exploding out of my shell and doing things I would never have contemplated in my younger years. Still I could not shake the nagging sense of unease. I continued to feel different from the people surrounding me, great people, but people around whom I could never be my true self.

It was around this time that Alex Haley's *Root* was televised in the UK. I was young, and still new to black culture, and hadn't yet received the history lessons of the experience of my ancestors. I was repulsed and mortified to learn, on screen, about chattel slavery in the United States; how could anyone write or broadcast a film on such a dehumanizing experience? Learning that this was not fiction, that this had happened, and for centuries no less—I will carry that with me forever. I vowed from that point to devote myself to black history, my history, and the culture that rose in its wake.

I was still struggling academically at the time, though. In high school I was placed in the upper stream class--the A stream --and hence surrounded by the brightest children in the year. I was blessed to attend a school that valued education for all, irrespective of the student's background or race. A value I hold close to my heart. This was great, however I struggled to keep up with them and often found myself at the bottom of this class full of the brightest students.

My teachers held high expectations of me. They would not let me give up, even when I pleaded with them to move me down to a lower stream class. I was tired of giving it my all only to remain at the bottom. I was embarrassed. I wanted to be among the top performers. I felt stupid. By contrast, my teachers saw something I didn't; they believed in my ability to achieve and refused to feed my fears. Instead, they provided the necessary support to boost my belief in my ability to learn. I stayed the course, kept trying and gradually moved up the ranks in my class. I'll never forget the day when we received the results of a chemistry test, a moment I had been dreading as I sat there, waiting. When I was handed my paper, I was shocked to find that I scored a high mark in the top 25 percent. I was ecstatic, in complete disbelief. This was the day, I now know, that my true belief in self started to form. My taste of victory spurred me to do well in my other topics. From that point onwards my grades improved across the board, my highest scores being in science and religious studies. I finished high school at the age of sixteen with a mixture of good and average grades.

I went on to higher education in order to obtain a more focused qualification in science. During these two years I wasn't quite sure what I wanted out of my career, other than that I yearned to work in a clinical environment in a hospital. I researched several career options during this time and none of them appealed to me. Nonetheless, I kept searching.

It was during this time of searching that I discovered my love of photography. I had taken courses in it during high school, and I had been developing my own film into black and white prints. I wanted a career in this: the mix of finding a visual subject, framing it in the exact way needed to evoke its power or beauty or truth, and then using precise technical skills to both take the photograph and develop it into a finished preservation of that moment was incredibly meaningful to me.

I joined a photography club, and began asking the older members about careers in the field. I even had an interview lined up with The London School of Printing. These older practitioners were united in one opinion: that I should pursue a different field, one that would provide me with a strong and fruitful career outside the scarcity of quality photography jobs. I heeded their advice and turned elsewhere, preserving photography purely as an interest or hobby.

During my renewed search, my academic advisor encouraged me to apply for scientific positions even if I felt I wasn't qualified for them. I didn't love science yet, by this time, my upbringing and the advice from various parties had me motivated to find solid professional footing, so the sciences felt like a strong bet. This effort and much needed guidance resulted in me being offered a research technician's job at the Royal London School of Medicine and an offer to attend Birmingham University to study Applied Biology. I was offered a place at the University first. I remember feeling relieved I had somewhere to go after college; I also remember having a strong sense of knowing this great opportunity was not for me. I was relieved but not excited. The prospect of moving to Birmingham, about eighty miles away from my family and friends, was not appealing. Soon after I received my offer, my mother was super excited about a phone call she received from a Professor Keating at the Royal London School of Medicine and Dentistry asking for me to contact him about a position in the physiology department. I was invited to interview for the position as a research technician, which I thought at the time I applied I would never get. I don't have much memory of the process or even the interview. I just remember receiving the offer and how excited and right this opportunity felt. The universe seemed to work it out as the date they wanted me to start fit perfectly with the time I would finishing college.

This was the first step in my professional career. At the London School of Medicine and Dentistry I emerged in an enriching, stimulating, and challenging environment of basic medical sciences in the physiology department. I worked with strong academics who taught me many lessons in life, and I discovered my love of science and the intrigues of the brain. Here I took steps toward becoming a scientist through technical on-the-job training. These were also the years in which I married and gave birth to the first real love of my life, my son Andrew, before getting divorced and four years later giving birth my second love, my daughter Portia.

At work I was encouraged to further my education and study for a graduate degree in Applied Biology one day a week while working the other four. This approach to learning worked well for me, as it became apparent I learned best by hands-on didactic approaches. Plus, I was surrounded by excellence and received additional support from the academics in my department. I excelled using this approach, and after five years of focusing on my studies and working I earned my first degree in Applied Biology, specializing in psychopharmacology. I got a good class degree, an Upper II, nearly the highest mark. I was proud of my achievements particularly because of my early academic struggles; the belief and perseverance I showed to reach where I now stood felt as affirming as any experience in my life.

Sylvia Bartley PhD

NEUROPHYSIOLOGY

Mortified and dumbfounded. _The likes of you pursuing a PhD is a mockery to the education system. What do you know about neurophysiology?_ I looked over at my colleague. She hung her head and avoided eye contact. _Tell me about the somatosensory pathways, what do you know about them?_ The taunts went on forever. They came from a privileged young, full-time PhD student with a private-education background in the third year of her PhD research and had started writing her thesis. She berated me in front of others I worked for, and was relentless in her reproach. I felt a deep wrenching feeling in my stomach; I walked away with my head down feeling embarrassed, stupid and inferior. I had no words for her. I didn't want to defend myself; part of me believed her.

I do not know what it was inside me that refused to give up. An inner drive was nudging me to stay on course, and I was out to prove to myself the perceived impossible was possible. My sixth sense nudged me forward and encouraged me to study. I knew, somehow, that the only response to such ridicule was to do what she said I couldn't. Maybe then I would be on equal footing with her and others who looked down on me or even pitied me for being me, a so-called disadvantaged black woman raising her children single-handedly with the support of her family.

I didn't know anyone with a doctorate at that time. Back in the eighties, there was a class divide. The academics considered themselves a higher class than the technical

30

staff, and it seemed clear that they wanted the world to think so as well. Not too long before I join the medical school, academics and technicians were actually segregated in the tea break rooms, and opportunities for technicians were limited to technical assignments. It was unusual, even unprecedented, for technicians to obtain a doctorate and cross over to the academic side. It was a mentality from "Upstairs, Downstairs," a popular British TV series about two different classes of people, an upper-class family who lived in their estate home while the hired help, their servants, lived downstairs. This was the prevailing mindset in academia and had been for decades one of the reasons for my reticence when I was asked to apply for a doctorate.

Deep down I knew this was an honor, but at the same time I had little confidence that I could achieve this high level of academic qualification. I didn't consider it before because I felt it wasn't for the likes of me. I felt inferior. In my early years in my job, I was reserved and did whatever was asked of me without question. Once I started to know my stuff I began to acquire the confidence to ask questions...only to be taken aback by how quickly I was put in my place, scolded or told never to question by some academics whom made it crystal clear to me that I was expected to do only as I was told, and not to wander past the strict parameters of my job. At this stage, I quickly complied; I still felt as though I didn't necessarily belong here in such lofty academic heights in the first place, and was fine with just attempting to blend in.

But there were other times far worse than that, crossing the line to where it was personally hurtful or downright insulting. There was an incident when I proudly showed a colleague--a very nice man by all accounts--an adorable picture of my one-year-old son on his birthday. I was so happy and proud of my handsome young man—and then floored when his response was, "he looks like he's going to mug someone already!" I was devastated. His insensitive, oblivious, cruel remark was utterly groundless, and I wondered why he viewed us in that way. I was all the more confused because he was otherwise very nice, and we got on very well. Yet he held this negative stereotype of my one-year-old son, or, more to the point, black people. It was difficult to reconcile that. It did not help my growing feelings of inferiority and difference.

This was not the only time that the undercurrents of racism running through the place emerged to the surface. On another occasion, I recall two of my female colleagues, my so-called friends, talking smugly about colonization, stating that if they, the white folks, didn't go over to Africa and colonize the continent, Africans or black people would not be civil or educated. It was their belief that white people educated black folks and black folks were uncivil; apparently, the uncivil and violent acts of exploitation and chattel slavery were for our own good. All of this was blatantly said in front of me with a high sense of righteousness. Did they expect me to share their bizarre point of view? Maybe they were expecting me to thank them!

A senior academic boldly told me that, if this had been many years ago, I would only be allowed in the building to clean the floors. This was a person I associated with at work. Such cutting remarks let me know what he really thought of me, and indeed, of all people who looked like me. He was nice to at times, however too often his true feelings would be revealed, usually once he got comfortable around me. All the while I had to work with him and others who no doubt did not consider me their equal.

I was not well enough acquainted with my history then, nor did I then recognize the strong shoulders of the ancestors that I stand on, to have the courage to stand up for myself. Not knowing who I was put me in a weak position to defend myself and my race. However, I intuitively knew their comments were wrong, insulting and degrading. Making matters even worse, some of my work colleagues also expressed their strong support of apartheid in South Africa, and spat disdain at me when I questioned why they would want to go there for a vacation. All this swirled around me while I pursued a PhD. I also didn't know as much as they did, since they had a much higher level of qualifications and different experience than me, which was particularly discouraging.

During my thirteen years at this institution there were many positive experiences too. My supervisor, Professor Michael Armstrong James, fondly know as MAJ, was one such example. He ignored the rhetoric and for some reason believed in my abilities to achieve higher academic qualifications. He opened the door for me, and once others realized I had the intellectual capability to learn neuroscience at their level, they took out all the stops to help me. Some even gave me the opportunity to teach.

Once again I grabbed these opportunities with both hands, eager to prove my critics wrong, including the biggest critic of them all, myself. I poured countless hours into preparing my lectures and sorting feedback from everyone, looking for ways in which I could improve them. For me, this was great fun. Teaching helped me grow; you only know what you don't know when you have to teach it. I would follow up with the students on questions I couldn't answer. I would ask my supervisors who unreservedly and eagerly shared their knowledge with me, and sometimes to my surprise they didn't have all of the answers themselves. When this occurred we looked it up together and discussed what we discovered. Then I would get back to the student or class with the answers, which they always appreciated.

My approach to teaching served me well later in my career, while working in the Operating Room for Medtronic with neurosurgical teams. I would study and do a run-through of the procedure workflow and technical operations of our surgical equipment. I would brush up on my neurophysiology and brain anatomy. Every day a new situation would arise, and I researched answers and solutions for the neurosurgeons. Over time my knowledge increased, and I became an expert in my field at Medtronic. I never pretended I knew all the answers, and my approach in seeking the correct answers and coming back with a comprehensive response helped me gain respect from the neurosurgeons.

Just like in the operating room, the department of physiology at the Royal London School of Medicine and Dentistry became an enriching environment for me. I flourished, learning more and more each day. Overall, my time at the Medical school was very positive and it laid the scientific foundation for the rest of my career. The kindness, genuine support, and friendships from the people that mattered to me overshadowed these negative experiences and the duplicity I sensed in some of my colleagues, and gave me hope and the will to continue along my path.

MAJ asking me to consider registering for a PhD was one of the biggest, boldest opportunities so far in my life. I mulled it over for a couple of weeks before I humbly accepted his offer. Our faculty of Basic Medical Sciences probably had an intake of around twenty to thirty or so full-time PhD students across all divisions. I distinctly remember listening to the woes of one student who had unsuccessfully applied for a grant to pursue a doctorate. What she would have given to grasp the opportunity I was offered. I heard this message loud and clear, and, filled with excitement and nervousness, I agreed to register.

I was mindful that MAJ was taking a risk. I was not the typical candidate for the program, not just because of my background but because I was a technician, not an academic.

As I considered the offer, I spoke to another supervisor, the same one I mentioned earlier, who also taught me well and who viewed me as disadvantaged black single parent. He had no qualms about offering this assessment frequently and quite bluntly. When I asked his advice, he told me directly, "I don't want you to pursue a PhD because I want you to remain my technician." His arrogance was so off-putting, he preferred to deny me the opportunity of a high-level education just to remain his subordinate.

At that moment I realized the power of education. It is the way in which people can find opportunities and reach their potential, but it can also be wielded as a tool of oppression. I think of the slaves again, and how the ruling class strictly forbid them from learning even basic literacy skills. By depriving these people of education, they kept them separate from what they were capable of, and from their own senses of self-worth; knowledge is power, and slavery and other forms of class-based oppression subsist when that power is kept from those who are oppressed.

I decided to ignore this man, and went ahead anyway. He for some reason (maybe out of spite for my upcoming advancement?) thought he was intellectually superior to me despite the fact that he, too, came from humble beginnings. Once again I was set on defying the odds, on doing what he felt I couldn't or just shouldn't do based on who I was.

Once, for some unremembered occasion, there was a gathering outside of work with the academics. After the event, the same supervisor and his wife planned to have a few people over to their home, which was located in the nice part of town. He went around the room to extend invitations, and when he came to my guest and me he gently told me I wasn't invited because I would be jealous of his beautiful home. I was deflated; yet again I was being told I wasn't good enough, or was too inferior to visit the man's house, this time in the presence of a personal friend who was also black. His wife overheard him, took him aside, and gave him what appeared to be a stern talking-to. He came over to apologize, inviting us to join the party.

I was humiliated, frustrated, and then incensed he had the gall to now invite us to his home. I rejected his offer, stating that I understood I was not good enough and I didn't want him to feel uncomfortable. He insisted, almost begged me to accept his invitation. I don't know what his wife said, but it was impactful; he looked truly remorseful. So I made him sweat a bit more before accepting his invitation. He was very hospitable when my guest and I showed up. He took us for a tour of his home and gardens. It was nice and there were no feelings of jealousy

I wonder why this man was put into my path. On one hand he taught me a lot academically, particularly the fundamentals of physiology, for which I'll always be grateful, but on the other hand he infringed on my dignity in ways so far beneath any code of decency. He tested me. I say "tested" because of a specific instance when he said something degrading and I challenged him. My work friend, a female colleague whom he respected and treated well, was present and challenged him further on his slurs towards me.

He responded by stating he didn't have any black friends and didn't grow up around black people, so he didn't know how to react towards me and wanted to see how far he could go—what my limits were. He was confused because sometimes I would not respond to his barbs, and other times I would. My friend politely told him that first of all I should be considered a human being, female second, and a black female last of all, if at all. Somehow, he'd never thought of it in that way. My friend's comments empowered me to express to him how his comments made me feel, and there were no further incidents; I think he may have actually learned a life-changing lesson that day, albeit one I would have hoped he and anyone else would have learned far earlier.

He was still one to jump on gender differences, and he created the first version of the schematic diagram that shows the different emotional responses to anatomical structures between genders, which I still see being used today. His negative attitude towards me lit a fire in me that has never gone out. Even though I felt it and I didn't like being told that I wasn't good enough, in seeking a way out of my situation, I was quietly driven to educate myself to the highest level possible.

I buckled down for five years and really focused on getting it done and getting it done well. Four months into my first year, I was runner-up for the faculty prize for the best doctorate research work; in my second year, I earned the accolade outright. Competition was fierce, with about sixty students ranging from those just starting out to medically qualified and trained doctors from prestigious medical schools pursing their final year of research.

MAJ returned from the faculty members committee meeting beaming. He told me the outcome, and explained why he felt this was a great achievement because of the high level of competition and the accolades he received on my behalf from other faculty members. This award gave me good visibility and exposure to the faculty members across the four major functions in our faculty: Physiology, Anatomy, Pharmacology, and Biochemistry.

Attitudes towards me changed after that success, and opportunities to engage in more academic-type work opened up. For example, I was asked to be part of an interview panel for an open position in one of the departments. This was my first experience interviewing and, true to form, I did my homework and sought counsel from friends who had this experience. I got a diverse view of best practices used to interview candidates and presented this at the preparation meeting with which the interview panel happily adopted. The head of the department nodded with approval when I made the suggestion on how we could conduct the interview, which we adopted and the interviews went smoothly.

I enjoyed this experience immensely. I felt confident in what to look for in a candidate, and how to ask probing questions to understand whether the candidate was a solid fit for the job. These types of questions were also designed to help the candidate understand whether the job was the right fit for him or her. My reputation grew, and this experience opened the door to more such opportunities. I was on my way.

It was unusual for a technician to transition over to academic activities. To my knowledge, only one man had done this before me. A female technician who wanted to do the same was unfortunately told this was not her path by a senior academic. She disagreed, telling him it was possible and using me as an example. He told her I was an exception to the rule; this would not happen for her! When she told me this, I was stunned. I was pleased that I was considered, in the truest sense of the term, "exceptional," but felt dismayed that my achievements weren't breaking down the barriers that stood in the paths of others like me.

What a contradiction: being both proud to be an exception to the rule while being equally frustrated that the rule existed in the first place. It was the feeling of wanting to achieve something notable in such a way that the people following my path would be considered ordinary. With that contradiction came a significant amount of pressure as well. The history of progress is riddled with people who "almost" got what they wanted, and then are cruelly and unfairly used as examples for why no one else like them should ever come close.

I did my best to ignore the weight of the situation; I had no extra energy to deal with these types of distractions. More important, I was hell bent on showing my children what can be achieved with hard work, perseverance and belief in oneself. At this stage failure was not an option.

Gradually, I began to see my potential and felt worthy of this opportunity. That dreaded monster of self-doubt and isolation steadily retreated over time, and the more physiology I learned and understood the more confidence I had in myself that I could do this.

Once I realized failure was not an option, I took this mentality to the next logical step and began visualizing my graduation. The impossible was now possible; I felt the elation of achieving my academic goal. I visualized my mother's beautiful smile as she attended my graduation, my young children watching me, in my floppy hat, receive the second-highest academic achievement in the ceremony; I visualized telling my father that I had achieved what he always wanted from his children—an impressively high-level education. These images were powerful, and whenever a doubting moment crept into my psyche, I visualized my graduation and the smiles of all the people who supported me along the way.

Throughout the duration on my studies, things were difficult. Even with the support of my family and friends, I struggled to make ends meet. I was driven and determined that my family and I were not going to become or remain a negative statistic. I was going to defy the stereotype that had been placed on me all my life. My children and I would beat the odds and live highly successful lives.

Of course, an intense time such as this can be incredibly formative for one's internal voice. Mine developed along with my defiance, and I became very accustomed to it, to the point that I could hear it and feel it egg me on. I now realize the voice was my internal spiritual guide. It's hard to describe what it actually is; there are no words spoken, no burning bush or a voice from above. I am quite certain that it's a feeling that's not generated by my thoughts or any physiological stimuli, instead coming from my soul. Don't ask me how I know this, I just do—that sense of knowing. It's deep, innocuous yet prominent at the most crucial times in my life.

I don't recall being spiritually aware at this stage of my life, but I do recall having repetitive dreams of a supernatural nature--dreams that put the fear of God into me and kept me on the straight and narrow. This was a time when my internal guides gently and clearly whispered words of encouragement; they willed me to overcome the obstacles placed in my path. What I heard was this: despite what people say, I would achieve my PhD, so ignore them, keep my head down, work hard and I would achieve my doctorate with flying colors. There was nothing to gain by listening to all of the negativity; it was crucial for me to learn how to tune it all out.

My children deserved opportunities to succeed in life, and I was determined to help them be in a position where they could apply to any college or university and ultimately attain the job of their choice. They inspired me to be successful in my academic quest. I wanted them to witness, to know and feel the power brought by a good education.

When it was time to submit my thesis and have my viva voce (*live voice*, or oral exams), I was a nervous wreck. I studied until my head almost exploded. I spent every waking moment reading, reviewing my work, and ensuring I was ready to answer any questions the examiners could throw at me. MAJ fought hard for me to have access to the computers and resources I needed to prepare, for which I'll always be grateful. I spent weekends in offices and libraries, ran around town to have the whole giant project printed. As this thing grew—in even the physical sense—so too did my sense of accomplishment. I was almost there. I could have cried when I saw it on printed paper for the first time; I was scared even to touch it.

All sorts of things were churning through my head, and as a result, when I carried copies my life's work in my hands across London to the binders, I feared I would either be mugged of my thesis, I would leave it on the Tube, drop it in a rain puddle, or countless other possible mishaps that might have destroy my work. Why was my mind playing these kinds of "what if" tricks on me? Perhaps it was that same emotional muscle memory as ever, that constant, bracing fear of something unseen sweeping in to leave me in shambles. Whenever I had gotten close to being happy or doing something I was proud of, my feeling of elation would be curtailed by an event that sent me right back to being deflated and unhappy. I was petrified of losing my work, work that could change my life's trajectory. I held onto those papers so tightly and close to my chest you would have thought I was carrying a pot of gold. To me it *was* gold. It was everything.

When I went to collect my five royal blue bounded books with "Sylvia Bartley PhD" in bold gold letters on the book's stem, I was in even more disbelief than before. It was official. I did it. Now I was only one step away from obtaining a doctorate in neurophysiology! I kept flipping through the pages repeatedly saying to myself, "You did this—you did it." I submitted two copies to my examiners with equal care and diligence while keeping the other three copies in the office.

The examination was held at another University in London. MAJ accompanied me. The approximately twenty-minute journey on the Tube felt like an eternity. We travelled in silence. Amongst the hustle and bustle of thousands of Londoners navigating their way briskly through the Tube, I could hear and feel my heart pound against my chest - heavy, slow and rhythmic. Each step I took, I knew that when I traveled this same route back to our university, I would be a different person, whether I failed or succeeded. I wanted to throw-up with pure anxiety—still I had to give one of the best performances of my life.

My internal examiner was an academic at the University, and so we arranged to meet in his office. In the UK, PhD students are examined by two examiners who are leading experts in the field of research you're exploring. One had to be internal, i.e. from the same city you did your research, in my case from a university in London (not the one you are from) and the other external to your city. During the viva you have to defend your research and be ready to answer any question they could ask you related to your work and similar research. I was prepared for a grilling. We found the office and I walked up the steps in a daze. I literally cannot recall anything about the building or the reception area. I just remember a very tall, stocky man opening the door and looking down on me with the gentlest, most compassionate eyes. In the background I saw a smaller shorter man, wearing a bow tie and tweed jacket who greeted me with a warm Scottish accent. They were at ease and I was a nervous wreck. The tall professor asked me, "How do you feel?" I immediately expressed my anxiety, and he looked me over and then said very clearly and almost lovingly, "Your work is excellent. Think of this as a celebration and not an examination. You have passed, so let's just have a good conversation about your research."

My head was spinning. Did he say I passed? Did he say I have achieved my Doctorate in Neurophysiology? I looked at the other examiner for reassurance, and his face told the same story. I sat down and waited for the "but," but it never came. I sat there in complete disbelief and elation. I managed to string a few intelligent sentences together with a permanent wide smile on my face, and they were satisfied with my summary and answers to their questions.

After about sixty minutes it was all over, no corrections, no uncertainty, just an outstanding "you passed!" Even now, years later, remembering this scene brings tears to my eyes. That powerful moment forever changed the trajectory of my life. I had known students to be grilled for up to eight hours in their viva and then asked to make several changes to their thesis before it was accepted. The average time for a PhD examination was three to four hours. Mine was over within an hour and in the last ten minutes we talked about my future plans. I floated out of there with a PhD in neurophysiology, elated, grateful and eager to get home and tell my family and friends.

On the Tube ride back to our university, dear MAJ gave me his parting words of wisdom. He said, "Now I will retire. I wanted to see you through this, and I am very proud of you. You earned your title. You have worked hard for it, and you deserve it. Some people won't like you using your title, but don't listen to them. Always use it: it's yours."

When we arrived back to our university, the physiology department faculty and others greeted me with champagne and celebratory wishes. They were jovial, smiling, laughing, hugging me and raising a glass to me. They lined up to congratulate me and tell me how proud they were of me and what a great achievement I had made. I had been there for thirteen years, and many of the academics had long tenures of two decades and more. We were like family now. We had grown close, getting to know each other quite well. We were open with each other, we challenged each other's thinking, and ultimately we respected each other. They respected me—their support was a major boost for my self-esteem—and more importantly, I knew how much they cared for me.

A couple of faculty members came up to tell me they had been skeptical in the beginning. In fact, they had told MAJ he was crazy to register me, and now we had both proved them wrong. They shared these details with good intention. MAJ never told me his judgment was being questioned—knowing these guys, I'm sure they gave him a lot of grief for supporting me. He never let on. Instead, he was hard on me, encouraging me to produce the best thesis ever.

I'm grateful to MAJ for his brilliance, for his kindness, and for his support when no one else wanted to give me the same opportunities they had. He demonstrated to me firsthand the meaning of transformational leadership. The power of education coupled with someone believing in you and your ability can change the trajectory of your life. I feel this responsibility to others, especially people in my community. Paying it forward is a must, and my responsibility.

When I received my PhD, my daughter was kindergarten age, old enough to proudly tell her teacher so. Both of my children went to the infant school I attended, and some of the same staff members were still there. Her teacher, who had also taught my son, was so proud of me. When

I came to collect Portia from school, her teacher stood at the door with smile beaming from ear to ear and said in front of the other parents, "Portia told me you got a PhD, congratulations—what is your doctorate in?" When I told her Neurophysiology, her smile got wider and she praised me again. She looked so proud, and all of this was in front of my daughter, some of her friends and their parents. They joined in the congratulations. I stood there feeling good, in some part for myself, but more because my daughter had witnessed her teacher and others praise me for my academic achievement. I wanted my children to know that we, black people, are not inferior, intellectually or otherwise, and no matter what your situation, you can defy the odds and successfully blaze your own path. Your circumstances do not determine who you are. They're simply the beginning of your story.

When the feeling of elation disappeared, the doubts still seeped in and there were times when it was unclear to me exactly what I was supposed to do with my doctorate. Even now there are days when I don't consider myself to be a neurophysiologist on the cutting edge of science—even though I may be. My accomplishment was due to hard work and perseverance and pure focus, not natural intelligence— though perhaps there's some of that too.

Why? What would make me think that way? Now I can clearly hear my inner voice telling me that this put-down betrays a lack of belief in myself. It's negative talk I should avoid; instead, I should be more accepting of my accomplishments and embrace them wholeheartedly. Then I hear the voices of those who have heard me downplay my role in one form or another, and they are asking, "How exactly does one stumble into a doctorate in neurophysiology from a prestigious medical school in London?" That's a good question.

I believe the attainment of my academic goals is part of my path. Earning a doctorate was certainly not something that I ever planned on doing, or expected to happen. How could this have been anything other than exactly what was meant to be? As I reflect on my beginnings—a quiet child growing up in a stern household, living in the wake of my brother's death—this path feels correct, the one I was led to by my spiritual guides. I took that studious nature and put it toward rigorous academic work, and took a battle with what I would soon learn was depression and turned it into a fascination with the brain itself. I felt certain my path was meant to cross uncharted territory, areas I would hope to make newly available for people like me.

This could not have happened without paying attention to my spiritual self. Strangely, the most critical aspect of my success in studying the brain was to make sure I was listening to my own. These two sides, scientific rigor and spiritual wellbeing, were becoming inexorably tied. They have remained linked for me ever since.

When MAJ retired I made a decision to leave the university as well. I instinctively knew it was time to move on and follow my desire to work in a clinical environment, teaching and working with hospital staff. I did something very unusual for me: I took a risk and left my job without having another job lined up. The university was going through tough times financially, so I took the opportunity to leave and take the voluntary severance. This provided me with some breathing room to look for a job. I worked as a temp in the Royal London Hospital in the cashier's department, a basic administrative job I hated but knew I had to do to provide a small income while I interviewed for other jobs. I was introduced by a recruitment agency to medical-device sales, and soon knew this was the career I wanted to pursue.

One feature of the academic life is that its structure is fairly well formed. When you set out to do doctoral work, you are blocking many years of your life off. While this is rigorous and requires intense focus, it also allows for routine, for developing a rhythm to life. It's a stage that removes many larger questions about whether we're in the right place, whether it's time to make a change, whether what we are focused on the correct things. Setting out into the professional world foregoes all of that. There are infinite variables and lots of uncertainty, from what city you'll end up making a life in to the people you end up surrounded by. I had come from a community at school in which I'd worked very hard to gain the respect I was owed; I would have to start that process again once I found a new job. More of the journey. I would find that there were people who were very hesitant to accept me into their professional world.

After several interviews with different companies I was offered a job at Medical Device Cardiac Company based in middle England, where I cut my teeth in sales. It was tough because most of my customers, cardiologists, didn't want to speak to me, much less use my product, because my company had less than 1 percent of the market share in my area of sales. I was out to prove myself, once again facing that same isolation and separateness that had come to define my life and work to this point. The underdog. The one they'd gladly do away with. Moreover, there were just a handful of people of color in these roles, and even far less black sales representatives and cardiologists. Regardless, I got on with it and quickly started to excel in my field, continually soaking in new knowledge like a sponge. At this stage in my life I thrived on beating the odds.

I kept showing up to my accounts on the day they did procedures, and waiting patiently in the corner of the catheter laboratory, learning their procedures and about heart disease. I would engage the physicians, asking them about the types of blockages they witness and how they make decisions. I discovered most physicians liked to teach, and I was a student willing to learn. My neurophysiology background was a conversation starter and gave me credibility, so they would eagerly teach me about cardiology.

At the time, I found cardiology fascinating because of the heart operation my son had; he had been diagnosed with the same congenital condition I had, a PDA, when he was four, and he too underwent surgery. However, with advancing technologies and practices, his procedure was not open-heart surgery like mine was. Using a minimally invasive vascular approach, a balloon was delivered to his heart, where it was deployed and expanded to close the hole. The procedure took an hour or two, and the next day my ex-husband and I were happily taking our son home.

It was one more unexpected turn in my journey and his; at the same time, it felt familiar. Heart conditions had resonance with me, having undergone open-heart surgery as a child. I had gone silent for nearly a year in the aftermath of the procedure; would my son be affected the same way? Having gone through such a thing myself, would I be more prepared as his mother to help him through the procedure? As I've said, I believe our souls undergo lessons and trials so we can evolve and better interact with those we are close with in this and other lifetimes. In this new turn my life had taken toward cardiology, I was seeing how I might be able to apply the lessons my soul had learned early on.

I distinctly remember going on a trip to our International Headquarters for a regional business meeting. This was my first business trip abroad. I was so nervous and excited; I packed everything except my passport! We were traveling together as a team and I was so embarrassed by this realization at the check-in counter. My manager was very gracious and handled the situation quite professionally, arranging for me to catch the next plane the following morning after I went home to get my passport.

When our sales results were reported to the international Headquarters I was told they questioned, or were very surprised to learn, that I was the one who was making a difference in sales and not the other members on my team. My question: Why were they so surprised? Unfortunately, I'm pretty sure I know the answer.

There was also the time when I was in a small team meeting and a person made a comment that shocked and humiliated me. My manager made a suggestion to the team and he piped up "we can't do that …it would be like looking *for a 'nigger in a woodpile.'*" He was sitting directly opposite me and turned red when he realized what he'd said. He blurted out a "Sorry, I didn't mean that." The people around me hung their heads and said nothing. My manager, who didn't hear him, asked, "Why, what did you say?" and he said it again followed by "I shouldn't have said it." My manager dismissed it and went on with the meeting.

I was furious. I expected her to defend me or reprimand him, but she didn't even acknowledge the insult—just an "oh" and a shrug of the shoulders. I hung my head and stared blankly at the table. I didn't utter another word. I felt humiliated, and once again isolated. There was no one in the company I could turn to for support, and no one who looked like me. I couldn't wait to get out of the office and start my three-hour drive home.

This had been the second time in my career I was confronted with this phrase. The first time was in academia, when a very senior member of the faculty staff used it in front of me and about eight other people, all white men and women. They also said nothing. One shifted in his chair but no one addressed it. After the conversation ended my female colleague acknowledged it and explained, "It's an old white-man term, he didn't mean anything by it." I said nothing at that time and went home mortified.

I felt weak for not speaking up and telling them it was insulting. He was a man who had the power to fire me. I thought about it long and hard considering my approach to addressing the issue. I spoke to one of my closer colleagues, a white male, who told me I shouldn't be upset, as this man did some charity work for the homeless so he must be a good person and this incident should not slight his reputation.

That phrase. It has its origin directly from slavery, together with the term *nitty gritty*. When a slave would die in the fields it was difficult for them to be found in the woodpile—hence the phrase. The *nitty gritty* referred to dealing with the most infested and sick slaves after their unimaginably cruel journey on the slave ships. When they docked they would take out the healthier slaves first and then would deal with the *nitty gritty* last. Granted, most people are ignorant of the true meaning of the latter phrase, however he never used it and he appropriately informed people, especially black folks, what it meant if they used the term.

After speaking with a friend who understood our history and who reminded me of those whose shoulders we stand on, and speaking with a black surgeon who assured me this was an open and shut case, I plucked up the courage to write that culprit a short and to-the-point note about his comments and my feelings. Maybe he would feel contrite about it and see the error of his ways—he wasn't. He was outraged. He came to find me, waving the note in my face asking me who put me up to it.

For some reason he didn't think I would take the initiative or have the courage to do so by myself. He tried to intimidate me by shouting at me and denying his words. He even tried to physically back me into a corner by walking up very close to me. He was a much shorter man, so I firmly stood my ground and reiterated the contents of my note. I found his comment to be insulting, offensive, and unacceptable. I requested that he refrain from using such a term in my presence again and if he did I would take more appropriate action. He was incensed.

Prior to sending him the note I had visited the Human Resource department and explained the situation to the lady in charge. I didn't want any action from them, but I was concerned about any potential repercussions. Hence I wanted them to be aware of the situation and the way I was going to handle it.

He left my office once he realized I wasn't in any way intimidated by his tactics. Afterwards, we would see each other more frequently than before in the elevator or corridor. He would growl at me or try and stare me down. I ignored him, smiled in public, and got on with my job. Funny enough, over time–many years–he came to respect me and ended up being a big supporter. He was the one who informed the other technician I was the "exception," and he had sent me the nicest complimentary handwritten note when I left the medical school. I treasured that note, as it meant a lot have our relationship take such a drastic U-turn.

So here I was again, in the same situation as before. I took the same approach, slept on it, sought advice and then addressed it with my manager. She was clueless, stating his term was not racist. I explained the meaning and questioned why she felt it wasn't offensive and her response incensed me even further. "I've never managed black people before so this situation is new to me." I didn't mince my words at this point, informing her of her responsibilities as a manager and the array of courses she should take to enlighten herself about diversity and inclusion. She acted as though it was my problem for simply being black. I expected better of her.

A few minutes after we spoke I received a call from the country manager. He couldn't apologize enough for the incident and my manager's response. He informed me of the policies on racial discrimination and/or harassment at work and asked how I would like to proceed.

The issue had surpassed the incident during the meeting. The culprit apologized, admitted error and we moved on. My issue was now with my manager's lack of sensitivity, or awareness on how to manage me. Hence I was quietly relieved when the opportunity came to work for Medtronic, a company with strong values, and a large market presence I admired in the Neuromodulation division. This area of work was much closer to my research and I could get back to brain science and learn more about it in the clinical setting.

Despite these challenges, I excelled at my first sales job and enjoyed the financial rewards when I achieved 100 percent or more of my sales target. After ten years of watching every penny I earned, I was finally in a position to take my children on a well-deserved vacation. I had been working twelve-hour days, not giving my children the full attention they needed. I wanted to give them a memorable vacation and booked a trip to Disneyland in Paris. My two children and I were excited; it was our first real vacation. Andrew was about eleven years old and Portia seven years old. It was their first time flying on a plane and visiting a different country. We stayed in the heart of Paris.

After a few days, I was low on energy and was developing a sore throat. I ignored it, willing it to get better so I could focus on my children as promised. They deserved the good time they'd been waiting for. I took some over the counter remedies for my throat and proceeded with a full day of tourist activities with the children.

It was the middle of August in Paris, unbearably hot and humid. The sun drained the little energy I had but I refused to ruin it any further for the children. We visited the Eiffel Tower, La Louvre to see the Mona Lisa, The Avenue des Champs-Élysées, Notre-Dame Cathedral, took a boat ride on the River Seine and enjoyed many of the other magnificent Paris attractions. Andrew and Portia took it all in, running around the sites, laughing, trying to speak French and happily eating the French cuisine.

I had to sit down at every opportunity I got as my health continued declining. The next day I woke up with an excruciating pain in my neck, and my pillow was soaked with saliva as it was painful to swallow. The hotel doctor prescribed antibiotics but it was impossible for me to swallow water much less tablets. Fortunately, my mother and sister had arrived for a few days and provided me with some relief, taking the children to Disneyland. As much as I wanted to I couldn't go with them and stayed in bed hoping to recover. At this stage I was miserable. My family had left and I was the sole person responsible for my children in my sick state in a foreign country.

I was weakened, and so it all finally hit me. The desire to connect with my children through quality time in this new place, the need to excel at this career I'd carved for myself, and most of all, the pressure of the constant quest to defy the odds and please everyone, including the vision I had for myself. I felt it dissolving as my body failed, having completely spent itself. I could barely even speak, and packing up so that we could leave early for London took whatever remaining strength I had left. I had broken down, finally. It had been a long time coming.

When we arrived home in London, I collapsed from pure emotional and physical exhaustion. Andrew called my mum for help and she came and took care of me and my children.

The next morning, I went to see my General Practitioner, who immediately sent me to a major academic hospital to the Ear, Nose, and Throat clinic. I looked like I'd taken a baseball bat to my mouth and throat. My jaws were screaming out in pain and when I tried to open my mouth, my throat was beyond painful. I was dehydrated. When I arrived at the hospital the doctor tried to pry my mouth open to aspirate the infection with a long needle and syringe. Sharp, intense waves of pain shot to my head. I became dizzy. I wanted to scream and shout at the doctor but I couldn't; instead, I cried. Even that was painful; it hurt my throat when I took the sharp intake of breath. I nearly collapsed.

The tears were streaming down my face and I was concerned about my children, who were in the next room. The doctor admitted me to a ward and I wrote down instructions for the nurse to call my mum to collect my children. Even though I was desperate to close my eyes and sleep, I couldn't until I knew they were in good hands. When I heard my mum's voice, I rolled over in the hospital bed and passed out.

I woke up with a drip in my arm containing saline, steroids and morphine. I was in hospital for five days followed by four weeks of recuperation at home. I was listless. I continued to have no voice for another three weeks or so—my mind and body were completely exhausted.

In a sense, this burnout was my soul joining with my body to tell me that corrections needed to be made. I'd been pushing so hard, in so many different ways, that I'd been forced to prioritize my external life over my spiritual self. I was able to get away with it for a while, similar to holding one's breath—but eventually our souls must come up for air, so to speak. My choices were either to slow down as a means of taking care of myself, or learn how to better maintain my spiritual side while moving at the speed my life required. The choice, in a sense, was already made. I wasn't one to slow down, even when my body screamed for me to do so. It was time to dig deeper into methods I could use to make sure my spiritual life was in order.

It was this during this period that I found my love for Deep Brain Stimulation (DBS) and all the wondrous benefits this therapy brings to the patients and customers. DBS therapy delivers chronic electrical stimulation to certain anatomical targets in the deep structures of the brain, primary for certain Movement Disorders in carefully selected patients. Electrical stimulation is delivered by an implantable pulse generator, just like a cardiac pacemaker, via two small leads that traditionally contain four spherical electrodes, precisely placed in the desired anatomical brain target.

The type of job I took at Medtronic was never advertised or even mentioned in my career office at school. I was unaware it existed and quite grateful that it found me. It was such an honor to work in this national role to support and train functional neurosurgeons in the operating room (OR) on the technologies Medtronic provides. I developed strong relations with many neurosurgical teams across the UK, and my knowledge of medical technologies rapidly increased. I found myself in radiology suites, observing magnetic resonance imagining (MRIs) and computed tomography (CTs) of people's brains.

My role soon expanded to Western Europe and the United States. I became an expert on DBS procedures and gained access to scientific congresses to learn about current thoughts and cutting-edge science in the field of neuromodulation. I took in a lot and still did not appreciate the power of what I was learning. Supporting DBS procedures became my life, and I viewed the therapy as normal. Yet, when I told folks what I did, I registered their amazement. They found it fascinating, which made me pause and question why. It had all become rather routine to me and I found nothing remarkable in what I was doing. I find the therapy remarkable. Perhaps a manifestation of my low self-esteem? Somewhere in the back of my mind, maybe I remained uncomfortable with my own success.

I enjoyed having the opportunity to travel extensively and to collaborate with the best neurosurgeons and physicians in the world, because eventually my role became global. These experiences opened my eyes to new possibilities, countries and ways of thinking. I became culturally diverse and fluid in my conversations. My children reaped the benefits of this as well, living in Switzerland and attending International schools where they made friends from all around the world, received a high-quality education, learned to speak French well and were exposed to new activities like skiing in the Swiss & French Alps and sailing in the South of France.

So what's not to love about my job at Medtronic? I work in an area I liked studying at school and I have opportunities that would never have arisen if it wasn't for my job. I'm on a path of continual learning, and my quest is to reach my full potential. I'm fortunate to have a career that aligns well with my core values, though this is hardly by coincidence: I now seek to align everything I do with my core values and spiritual awareness. My work sparks energy for me even when I'm exhausted; I'm always inspired to give it my all.

Progress, I was learning, was a complicated idea. I was pushing myself at a breakneck pace toward all the things I believed I wanted, that I had set out for myself as necessary to obtain. I had fought for and won the academic credentials, and had used them to establish a career for myself. I had children whom I loved, and who loved me. I had entered into a world that would have happily seen me fail and had instead put together a life that matched the external vision I had for myself. Each item crossed off a list I thought would amount to happiness.

This sort of external progress, though, could not have come without subjugating what was inside me. This is easy to see in retrospect: when feelings of hurt or humiliation or self-doubt crept up, what choice was there but to repress them so that they would not stand in my way? As a neuroscientist, I should have known then what I know now, that compartmentalizing and repressing in such a way is rarely as clean and orderly as we think. My spiritual self was suffering during these years and I was choosing not to listen, all part of an internal sacrifice I felt willing to make in pursuit of the materialistic world. It was not until I obtained the world that I saw the damage I was doing to myself. It was time to reopen my spiritual self, the part of me I had once valued so highly; the experiences to come would make that abundantly clear.

PART II

THE SPIRITUAL

I've been told numerous times how unusual it is for a person with my scientific background to believe in the power of the universe, past lives, the journey of souls, and other aspects of the so-called paranormal or supernatural. Raised in the Catholic faith, I've always believed in God. I still do. However, I never felt comfortable committing myself to any one religion and always had a burning need to learn about other spiritual practices. As I explored various beliefs, none resonated with me. I'm a scientist, and those habits present themselves in my spiritual life as well; I was compelled to keep searching, experimenting, until I found a place where my soul felt at ease.

I now consider myself a spiritual person, not a religious one. I'm open to being connected to the universe. I'm self-aware, able to tap into my inner self to be guided by my multi-senses and my spiritual guides. I believe in past lives and have taken action to learn about my own and the relevance they have for me today. I believe in the journey of souls, how they over time to reach a greater alignment with the universe. I'm not constrained by the system of religion; rather, I'm open to receive God's message through many channels. Even though there is no scientific proof to support past life regressions or the words of a trusted mystic, I believe wholeheartedly in the power of these nonconventional ways, together with traditional prayer, to connect with the universe and align with one's true path and purpose.

My definition of spiritual has evolved. It's about being enlightened, getting engrossed in the moment, focusing on the power of now, the power greater than us mortals, the power of the universe and the energy it emits to guide us through our journey in this lifetime. Being present, being aware of one's connection to the universe, is an indispensable component of spirituality. My goal to have a strong personal connection with the universe requires constant focus on my thoughts and being mindful of my intentions and subsequent actions. It also means consciously seeking to align with my true path and purpose, connecting with nature, and recognizing my calling and living it with compassion and humanity. I've seen firsthand the power of an enlightened soul, the beauty of being present.

For almost thirty years now, I have had a recurring dream of some dark force trying to suck the life out of my lucid self. In the dream, I'm lying in bed and this seemingly dark force enters the room from above, paralyzing me with fear. I always intuit that the force is evil. I resist mightily, as hard as I can, praying hard, but my mouth becomes paralyzed with the rest of my body. I lay frozen, pinned down by this strong force. Sometimes I wake up with a shudder, breathing heavily, and other times, after much effort, I quickly recite the Lord's Prayer and hope the force goes away. And it does.

I had this dream for years, in my many different houses. I never shared it with anyone. Having been raised Catholic, I just assumed that it came because I had done something wrong; it felt like I was at fault. As I got older and the dreams persisted, I began seeking answers. Finally, I spoke about it with a friend, Michael, someone I fondly think of as my "earth guide." Michael introduced me to Deepak Chopra's law of intention and his book *The Seven Spiritual Laws of Success*, which led me to Louise L. Hay, the godmother of spirituality. Her book *You Can Heal Your Life* helped start my process of spiritual healing through painful experiences.

Even after I had just met Michael at an event in Geneva, it seemed I'd known him forever. I felt comfortable with him and was able to share my dreams without fear or apprehension. I was keen to understand why this dream plagued me for so many years. He looked at me intently as if he understood, and then he posed a different angle for me to examine. "Why do you think the force is evil?" he asked. "Why don't you just ask it what it wants from you? Ask who it is."

By then he knew that once in my house in Switzerland, I had had the dream, but it had ended differently. What I would describe as a dark force distinctly shifted into a different realm, a calmer, lighter, peaceful place. Then I heard a warm, welcoming voice, a male voice that said, "Hello." I remember it like it was yesterday. It scared and surprised me; I jumped out of my lucid state. The place, so tranquil, was clearly on a different plane of existence. I wasn't mature enough in my spiritual journey at that point to recognize that a guide was connecting with me; I innocently thought it meant I would finally meet a decent man, a man meant for me.

I told this story to Michael, and he advised me to ask the question regarding the nature of the force approaching me. In one of his own dreams, a spirit appeared to him and he asked this question, and had a discussion with it. This whole experience was powerful: someone else understood my experience, and I had confirmation that my dreams did not mean I was crazy. I went to bed that night eager to dream again. It took a couple of nights, but the force returned. I was petrified as always, paralyzed for a while, and I could barely ask the question, but I did. The dark force shifted to something a bit lighter, and then it would go away or I would wake up before getting any answers. I remained perplexed by the whole situation.

Over time, as I've become more aware and open, I've realized my guides were trying to connect with me from an early age through my dreams. I still don't fully understand why, but I'm comfortable with the belief that the dreams or the guides are meant to put me on the right track to understanding my soul's contract—my purpose.

I was keen to learn more, so I read many books; in fact, for the last eight years I have read only spiritual books. Gary Zukav's *The Seat of the Soul* is my bible, providing me a foundational understanding of spirituality. I've read it numerous times, and in each encounter I glean something different from it. Michael Newton's *Journey of Souls* pushed me to the next level, answering many questions I had held inside for years.

Although I was brought up Catholic, I never understood or felt connected to that faith. I didn't believe in traditional conceptions of the afterlife. I feared death because I didn't understand what would happen in heaven, hell, or purgatory. I saw church as an artificial institution, like other religions, and thus fallible. Too often we witness dismaying acts committed in the name of religion. Chattel slavery is a prime example, and we all know how barbaric this practice is and the horrors it imposed on Africans for centuries, with damning effects on Africans in the diaspora even today.

I'm not tied to any denomination. When I sought out other faiths, I felt the same: the teachings were man-made, involving selective reading and misinterpretation of scripture. Michael Newton's writing helped me understand the concept of the soul's journey across many lives, each life focusing on a specific lesson which we chose in order to help our souls heal and evolve to the next level of spiritual awareness. This belief makes perfect sense to me. The idea of our past lives was new, but I readily understood that we were here before as part of our soul's evolution; we have soul groups—hence the phrase "soul mates"; we are here to learn how to have an impact on others. We chose our parents; our parents chose us. We signed up for it, in the choices our souls made in prior lives that led us to this current one. It gives me great pleasure to know my two beautiful babies, Andrew and Portia, chose me. Once, after Portia and I spoke about a disagreement we'd had and the resolution we'd reached, she said with pride, "This is the reason why we chose each other." I just love that she, too, is aware.

Michael is definitely in my soul group; that's why being together is so easy. Once, as we drove to Cully from Geneva, I said to this fifty-seven-year-old Dutch man, "I feel so comfortable with you." Sexual attraction had nothing to do with the pleasant feeling I had for him. He looked at me intently like he does and said, "That's because we have known each other in our past life." The penny dropped.

The concept was being introduced to me for the first time, but I immediately got it. Then Newton explained it all with his case studies. I was encouraged to continue reading and search for answers. During this process I was open, ready to learn. When the student is ready, the teacher appears—isn't that the saying? Well, teachers started appearing from all over: almost everyone I interact with now is an advanced spiritual being, on a journey to be enlightened and awakened. It's amazing. Zukav defines spiritual friends as those who support you without judgment, those who approach you from a place of equality and compassion. These are whom I seek, and whom I've been lucky enough to find. Along with a heightened sense of spiritual awareness comes an awareness of others as well; I want to understand their journey and purpose, and help them understand mine. This means that I want deep relationships, spiritual ones, which some people are not willing to give. It's fine when they don't; it simply means I can pour my attention and engagement to others who will.

Newton's follow-up book, *Destiny of Souls*, is equally powerful. It took me a while to pick it up, but when I did it cracked me open emotionally. One night, upon reading a certain chapter, I cried for what seemed like hours. Concerns I had carried with me for years about my father all came rushing out.

For more than thirty years my mother, who probably carried the heaviest load, remained supportive of her husband. My mother is patient and generous. I love her dearly, and I'm grateful that she protected my sisters and me from the harshness of life at home and in the world. She gives back tremendously to the community through her work at the church. For as long as I can remember, she has dedicated countless hours to helping with church operations as well as visiting hospital patients who, for whatever reason, have no loved ones to care for them. They are grateful to have someone to talk to them, pray with them if needed, or just sit with them. My mother is an angel. She received a certificate of dedication and gratitude from the Vatican— she was so pleased and we were so proud of her. Clearly, it is from her that I have derived my sense of community.

Destiny of Souls made me realize that I dreamed about my father daily for a reason: he was there because we have unfinished business. He didn't hate me, as I had felt he did for my entire life; he loved me, and moments when he showed affection toward me came flooding back. The night of these revelations was so emotion filled. I'd never cried like that before. Streams of tears and streams of anguish were released, and since then I've been more emotional, releasing the pain I've carried with me from childhood and perhaps over many lifetimes.

Given these details, one might logically ask: Why did I choose my parents? Was it to force me to this place of inner examination and the continual search for inner peace? I was quite introverted during my childhood. As I'd mentioned previously, my mother told me I refused to speak for a whole year after I had heart surgery. I don't remember the whole experience. Nonetheless, despite the holes in my memory, this part of my life is relevant today as I spent time in Operating Rooms working with surgeons and their teams. I greatly respect and admire all the surgeons I've had the pleasure to work with and learn from. I endeavor to support their profession in any way I can. My life is connected to these talented people and to the heart surgeons who helped me—and my son.

As we've seen, my life had become very external, and far too outward-facing for someone as naturally spiritual and inner-focused as me. In the past, particularly during my childhood, I found solace in prayer, particularly the more formulaic and Catholic kind I was being raised to appreciate. But I needed something different now. Something that felt more cohesive with these new spiritual ideas I was having, with my concept of guides and the journeys of souls. Catholic recitation simply wouldn't accommodate these truths, these feelings. It was time for new tools.

I learned how to meditate in Switzerland. Prayer has always been a part of my life, but meditation was challenging because my mind would not be still. Guided meditation helps to provide the structure I needed to focus. In its simplest form, that's what meditation is: concentrating on being still and tapping into the silence between one's thoughts. The science behind it is elementary. We concentrate hard enough or long enough to direct more blood to the prefrontal cortex, the part of the brain that deals with consciousness or our state of self-awareness. Here our positive and negative thoughts are created and reside.

Anything that helps you to focus, to tap into the silence between your breath—listening to music, exercising using rhythmic repetitive patterns, walking at a steady pace for a long period of time—will prepare you for mindfulness meditation. My best times for meditation are after I finish a hard session in the gym or a long run. In the gym I always engage in intense cardio workouts. Focus comes easily for me then because concentration has prepared my brain for this activity.

In Switzerland, I lived about three hundred meters from Lake Geneva and enjoyed a spectacular view of the lake and the Alps from my rental home. I had little understanding about vortices, or areas in which spiritual energy is highly concentrated, at the time, but immediately I felt the positive energy of the mountains. I would wake up every morning and be greeted by their presence, as they stood in their glory either with the greenness of summer or wearing crowns of ice and snow in the depths of winter. I was unable to describe or even begin to comprehend the strange feeling at the time, but now I recognize it was the upflow of energy from this minor vortex. The energy acted as my gateway from the universe, that greater plane of existence, to my personal energy spots, my chakras.

As it turned out, I was in Switzerland for good reason. At a shop up in Montreux, a little Swiss lady who was tuned in to the mountains and the energy they emitted gave me regular massages. She would check my chakras and work to unblock them and redirect my energy to areas of the body that needed it, bringing a sense of physical and mental well-being. After each massage she would tell me to look after my heart or would gently, lovingly offer some poignant words of wisdom. While she was alerting me to my inner needs, I did not realize her contribution at the time. I only knew her massages were wonderful. I have not found a masseuse like her since. I felt relaxed and at peace when I left her, immediately entering into a deep sleep and feeling refreshed when I woke. She was another earth angel guiding me along my path. Michael introduced me to this gentle soul, and I know I will be blessed to have her again massage me and balance my energy levels when I'm in Switzerland again.

I regularly ran along the lake and through the vineyards, the mountains in full view. I finished on what I called my bench by the lake, close to where many people walked and children played. Even as activity hummed happily around me, I would sit there for several minutes, gazing in awe at the Alps, the lake, the birds, the boats. At peace, I could meditate for long periods of time. Now I recognize that I was having an awakening experience. I could hear every sound of nature, see the real effects of the ripples of the lake, watch the swans and the birds flying high but I didn't register the sounds of people. I was in my world. I would be at peace knowing I was in God's presence, witnessing His beauty in every form.

I miss those times by the lake in Cully. When I return to Switzerland for work, I take time to be with the mountains. Regardless of the season, they stand magnificent and proud with presence and grace. We can all learn from the mountains and the energy they emit. Their vortices offer a spiritual connection—something Native Americans appreciate, as I recently discovered while here in Minnesota. Through my community, I've met a couple of Native Americans from the Dakota tribe, to whom I was immediately drawn. They have a calming, peaceful spirit and spoke knowingly of the earth's powerful energy. I felt connected to them for reasons unknown to me.

Native spirituality has always fascinated me. On a business trip in Scotland, I met a Native American person in a hotel breakfast room. The brief encounter was unforgettable, and not merely as acknowledgement of two people of color in a hotel. It went deeper, sparking a curiosity about spiritual beliefs. This person briefly showed up in my world at that time to remind me to seek out shamanic understandings and connections with the earth's energy, part of my path and journey. I clearly remember his spirit and strong presence in that room. Our eyes locked for a spilt second, and something resonated spiritually with me.

As I've described, I'm a prolific dreamer, with some of those dreams being lucid and some not, but I remember much of them. I have read Robert Moss's *Shamanic Dreaming for Healing and Becoming Whole.* The shaman belief that lucid dreams contain messages from the spirit world intrigues me. My dreams are so jumbled up I can't decipher the messages most times; however, I do believe in this concept. The sporadic nature of my dreams does not take away from their meaning and impact on me. I have dreamt of past lives and clear messages, images and warnings for my current life. My dreams, I believe, are a central way through which I come into contact with my spiritual guides.

I often see the face of the Native American man in Scotland when I read about shamanic dreaming. He was dressed in his traditional clothes, and I instinctively feel he was a shaman. I have no idea why I would know this detail or why I even remember him after our very brief encounter more than fourteen years ago.

A similar awakened experience came to me a few years later after a lengthy, intense work trip in Japan, followed by a national sales meeting in Arizona and then immediate departure to my last leg in Puerto Rico for another large meeting. After this grueling two weeks of travel, I was exhausted. My sinuses were completed blocked, my head was bunged up, and I was physically drained of all energy. Even so, I talked myself into being in the moment. After all, Puerto Rico was new to me, and it is such a beautiful place.

I was merely a participant in the meeting, required only to show up to the sessions. My hotel room had a direct view of the beach. The waves crashing on the shore were loud, rhythmic, and peaceful. This soothing song of fresh nature immediately sent me into a deep, peaceful sleep. I lay on my back with my head propped up high with pillows, mouth open so I could breathe and allow the sound to wash over me as I slept.

I woke feeling transformed. My sinuses had cleared, the pressure in my head had dissipated, and my body tingled in the intensity of the sunbeam from the window. I felt light to the point of floating, present to the point of peace. I scrambled for something, anything to write on.

On the hotel notepad I tried to capture the feeling, that lightness of being that felt as though it connected me with the nature all around me. I felt the ocean's waves wash across my heart; the sun's warmth radiated within me. The birds singing out my window were singing my song, praising their existence as I praised mine, sitting here by the window in the beauty of God. The sounds built toward crescendo as my spirit climbed, and I reached elation in harmony with the rhythms of nature.

Such experience is what I seek in my life; this uplifting sense of presence is the purpose of all the pain. Suffering led me to this point of pure elation, for you can only fully appreciate the light when you have experienced the dark. At that moment, I was completely present, basking in God's glory. My intention is to return to this state as often as possible, to be fully present always.

Despite this awesome experience the challenges persist: it's an ongoing journey. I have fears and uncertainties about how I exist in this world. Yet I also realize that the physical and emotional flaws I see are my own creations. I fully understand FEAR as an acronym: False Expectations Are Real, or False Evidence Appearing Real. Spiritual thought leaders warn against fears, and still I have them and they contribute to my reality. Day by day I need to work on reconciling my negative thoughts with positive chatter, allowing my protective, rational thoughts to point out all the reasons my negative perceptions are not real. It's pretty powerful stuff.

I first came across this practice many years ago in a book called *Mind Gym: Wake Up Your Mind* which offers practical exercises designed to counter hurtful chatter with questions about reality, questions that prove the negative thoughts to be untrue. Now, after years of practice, the positive chatter happens unconsciously. However, it's a continual journey, and there are days when the voice of reason is overturned by the doubts I have about myself. Regardless, I do believe my focus on evolving spiritually is having an effect; even if I can't see it, others can. What I feel on the inside is not reflected by how others view me on the outside.

Further, I am surrounded by spiritual beings asking similar questions of me, which only enriches my thoughts even further. The reading materials some of my friends send me are often quite deep and thought provoking. These folks are most certainly on a higher plane, and I strive to join them there. Indeed, that's why I surround myself with them. People are placed in my life for a reason. They may not be there for long, but they come with an important message I can clearly hear and understand. I consider these people to truly be light beings, messengers who appear at just the right time.

I've had many of these experiences, including recently when I was in Spain to observe a brain procedure. Seeing my colleague and observing her joyous state jolted me out of my negative self-talk. My colleague, a beautiful, radiant lady beaming from the inside out, is a living example of how to focus on being present. I was aware she had some health issues that categorized her as "disabled." But this assessment was in name only: her disabilities did not in the least prevent her from living life to the fullest. It was clear to me she was at peace with herself, and the only thing I saw was her beauty. You had to look hard to even notice her disability, because her radiance shined through, she did not focus on it. I was reminded that despite how I show up or what flaws I think I have, life is for living in the now. If I focus on the negative, that's what I'll draw attention to; however, if I focus on all of my blessings instead, that's what I'll draw people to, and they will see the beauty of me from within. A level of peace with myself translates into positive, high-vibrating energy, which by nature attracts the same around me. Low-vibrating energy takes work and distracts from doing positive things. I'll focus instead on all the positives and on being present, grateful, and at peace.

In 2010 I went to Bali, Indonesia, for a dear friend's fiftieth birthday. During the trip I felt compelled to find a spiritual priest to help me work through some strong internal feelings. I could feel those old ghosts of isolation, difference, a lack of belonging, and so I knew I had to visit a guide. After many days of following the crowd, something inside pushed me to have a day geared toward myself and my own spiritual needs. That meant finding a priest. I spoke with a nice man in the hotel in Ubud, a traditionally cultured town in the heart of the rain forest. I kept explaining what I wanted until he somehow understood my needs, perhaps even better than I did.

He drove us to a remote place, a small commune, and there a young spiritual priest (I'm not sure what else to call him) read me, checked my chakras, and performed a past-life regression. Then the priest prepared a cleansing ceremony for me. It was an unexpected and strange experience. He did not speak English, and we communicated through the hotel guide. They asked me to go into a room, remove my clothes, and wear a long robe (I cheated by keeping my underwear on), and when I saw the vessel filled with water, flowers, herbs, and other healing compounds in front of the temple (almost all homes in Bali have temples in the center), I knew I was about to get soaked. The priest sat ne down on a stool and slowly emptied the whole vessel of water over me, praying intently but gently all the while.

The experience sent me writhing: I couldn't breathe, my chest was heavy, and I felt like something was trying to force its way out of me. It was strange, uncontrollable, surreal— and it happened in the middle of the commune in front of other people, including my friends. I remember smelling the flowers' sweetness, feeling the pressure in my heart. Unaware of my movement, I marveled at my reaction to having water poured over my head. After the blessing, the priest said a few prayers and placed oils and rice on my forehead. I felt subdued, turned inward, for a few days afterward. This experience continues impacting me today. It unblocked my chakras and helped me be open to receive more from the universe. Writing about it now gives me goosebumps. I've evolved a lot since this experience, and I believe it helped set me on the right path. I now know for sure that it was the real reason I went to Bali.

I now seek solace from people in Minneapolis. A friend does healing and energy work on me when I'm feeling funky. I have built this healing practice into my lifestyle. When I'm on the table, she connects with my spiritual guides, who deliver messages through her. Some of those messages don't make sense at the time, but several months or even years later I come to understand. I record our discussions and the guidance given, and every time I read these notes I receive something different.

Nontraditional practices are now a big part of my life. It's so very interesting how energy works. A few years ago, I was a completely different person, a nonbeliever who never would have imagined I would end up here, on this spiritual journey. It is not as though I have all the answers; far from it, I still have lots of unanswered questions. There is one question that haunts me most.

During tough times in particular, I wonder: Why do we, our souls, need the human experience in order to evolve to the next spiritual level? The concept of soul groups— explored in Michael Newton's *Journey of Souls* and *Destiny of Souls*—resonates with me. The concept of guides working with our souls to help us evolve also makes sense. In the devout Catholic household of my childhood, the concept of heaven and hell was imposed upon me from an early age, but it never made any sense to me. If God is good, why would he allow for the possibility of eternal damnation? And the idea of receiving a "verdict" on one's own soul, of receiving a Final Judgment that determines where we spend eternity, also strikes me as impossibly harsh and artificial. And what am I supposed to make of Purgatory, a place in which souls are supposedly purged in preparation for heaven?

Until I was introduced to the concept of a soul's journey, I feared death. The thought of residing in a place forever scared me. I have instead been convinced and have come to believe in the evolution of souls.

Souls, I believe, are paired with lives and experiences designed to help it and other souls expand, to reach a higher level. All our souls have assignments, meant to help us understand the necessary growth that must take place before that next level can be reached. This is how our souls mature. We undergo trials that will expand the better parts of our nature while reducing the negativity and falseness that come tied into our egos. Evolved souls can exist almost entirely apart from ego; they're calm, peaceful, and able to focus on helping others reach the same state.

And so I think, again, of my brother Anthony, taken from us at only fifteen months and lost when I was just four years old. I question Anthony's purpose, his soul contract. What lesson or good came from his death? How did his short time on this earth help us? What was his contract all about? Did he really need this human experience? Did it help his soul to evolve, or was his purpose to help the family he chose to be born into? I wonder where his soul is now, how he has evolved. The thought of him sitting in heaven (because he was a pure young soul) seems reasonable. However, the thought of him being welcomed home, comforted by his soul group, and redirected to another lifetime warms my heart more. Wherever he is, I know he must be a gentle, evolved, loving soul by now.

I wonder what he would be like today if he had remained in this lifetime longer than those fifteen months. I'm sure we would have had a wonderfully close relationship. This example leads me to question the human experience: What is it about? Why does growth come with pain and suffering?

I've realized that when we learn to sit in the suffering, absorb the pain, and feel our human experience, only then can we truly be compassionate to others; suffering is a universal experience that allows us to understand each other, connect to one another on a spiritual level. This is my interpretation of groundlessness, a Buddhist concept that resonates with me. I came to appreciate this belief through Pema Chödrön's masterpiece, *Living Beautifully with Uncertainty and Change*, another book I refer to as my bible. During tough times over the last few years, I allowed myself to stop resisting and to sit in the pain to its full extent—to be groundless.

For me, emotional pain is far worse than anything that could happen to my body. We can often treat physical pain, no matter how severe, using principles and methods that come from science and medicine. Emotional pain is far more amorphous, complex, and hard to pin down, and so for this I have had to turn to the Buddhist concept of groundlessness. Thoughts whirl in my head, impossible to control. When

I stop trying, stop resisting, and just let them be, the pain subsides. My mind tunes into my third eye, my multisensory system, and I let it guide me to a place of peace. I have greater access to my guides and to a different realm that pulls me out of my state of mind and carried me through the painful moments. During these times, I have my deepest spiritual experiences.

My soul needs healing; I sense I'm carrying around the weight of sadness from one of my past lives. Hence my desire to learn about my past lives, to understand which parts of them are relevant to my experience today—so I can start the healing process and be at peace with myself. "How do you know your soul needs healing?" a friend asked one afternoon over lunch. The perplexed look on her face made me laugh until I cried. But hers is a serious question. How I know is unclear to me; I just do. Working with my energy healer, has provided some much-needed relief. While I don't fully understand the process of what's occurring, I feel lighter and unblocked. I typically see her when I reach the point of exhaustion or feel a deep sense of sadness for no apparent reason.

My friend Mary is a certified healing practitioner. Her work is based on the kinesiology concepts of working with meridians and chakras. She adopts a holistic approach, examining my state of well-being first by asking probing questions, seeking to understand the reason I came to her. After delving deep, we transition to the table. I experience a huge sense of relief as I lay there, trusting her, knowing that my soul will be well cared for. I zone out for a couple of hours, and when I wake up and leave the table I feel different, lighter and more at ease. Then she tells me what she saw, what she felt, and what my guides have said. She's a spiritual communicator.

Some people who know me will be very surprised to learn that I believe in the practice of spiritual healing. People see a corporate person when they look at me, a career neuroscientist. These things don't often come paired with spiritual practices. I can't tell you how much of a relief it is to leave the table and hear about my past lives through her. The process validates what I'm feeling and provides me with a quiet level of confidence about who I am.

Most of the healing practices adopted today are based on Native American traditions, incorporating mind and body techniques to treat psychological and physical conditions. The principles of Native American healing are based on the concept that spiritual imbalances are the causes of illness; these imbalances can be corrected by herbs, meditation, and rituals. I am curious about Native American practices even though I haven't attended a ceremony yet. The man I saw in Scotland sparked my curiosity. I can't help but wonder why he appeared in my life and why he is stuck in my mind. Maybe he was meant to guide me in the direction of seeking and ultimately adopting these spiritual practices. Maybe it was because our people share a familiar story. One thing I know for sure: I need to explore or seek healing practices more often. These are the practices that help me make sense of the world, and grapple with my pain. They're what I hope lead me toward further knowledge of myself and my circumstances. They teach me.

Life lessons can be very hard. Why do we need the human experience for our souls to evolve? Further, why does this evolution to the next level need to be so painful? I kept asking this question, and another dear friend, a Reverend, told me to stop asking. Why did I need to know, she wondered? I should just accept that this is what I signed up for. Well, that's an answer, and there is truth in that response. We all chose this human experience.

A session with my healing friend Mary brought confirmation: stop resisting. Our purpose is to understand our soul's contract and try to fulfill it in this lifetime. Sometimes this task is painfully hard, but the more painful the experience, the more I become awakened. As Mary J. Blige sings in her album *Stronger with Each Tear*, "With each tear there's a lesson, makes you wiser than before, makes you stronger than you know." The challenges come when I'm not focused on my purpose. I often want to live for my immediate ambitions and desires, and not my soul's contract; therefore, it doesn't work out. When I keep pushing, forcing what's not supposed to be forced, the painful experiences happen. When I ignore those signs, the experience becomes so hard, so painful, I have no choice but to stop. Because I'm hard of hearing at times (as my mother used to say), I need that big knock to bring me to my knees and put me back on track. And boy, have I had my knocks, and yes, they put me on this track of searching for answers.

Witness people are in my life for a purpose. Their path seems seamless to me. Their beauty shines from within, and they practically float through the world. The universe opens up for them and things move in their favor. They are living "on purpose."

I can recognize my on-purpose moments. A simple example is when my daughter Portia and I moved from Switzerland to the United States, things definitely worked in my favor to make a smooth transition. The opportunity to move came in July, and I agreed to relocate at the end of August so Portia could start school at the beginning of the school year. Our visas arrived in record time. I found a school and was able to assess it in person before relocating. I easily sold my home in the United Kingdom and purchased one in the United States in the desired school district. My furniture shipment, which typically requires three to four months, arrived two days after I got the keys to our new home, and my plants survived the long boat ride from Europe. Many more things aligned in a timely fashion, all pointing invariably to the conclusion that I had made the right decision. More important, when I walked into my new home for the first time, my spirit whispered, "welcome," and I exhaled a sigh of relief.

Should I stop questioning and just accept what I've signed up for? How can I spiritually evolve and be more in alignment with my path and purpose? Why do I feel the need to access different realms to be at peace? Is this part of my purpose? I have on occasion connected with my guides during my dreams, and they brought me to a peaceful, calm, tranquil place. This experience together with other signs and signals indicates what's in store for me.

I seek answers in many books on spirituality. The authors deeply exploring this topic are given real exposure when they appear on Oprah's Super Soul Sunday. Here I discovered many spiritual leaders, everyday people who have found their quest in life to spread the word through their experience. It's a movement I would gladly join. However, my journey seems a bit different. Everyone's purpose is unique. I return to my feelings of being on the outside looking in, seeking where I fit in, who my people are. I'm now meeting folks who align with my thinking, like-minded people on a journey toward fulfillment and inner peace.

However, I'm also meeting people who appear to be aligned but then back off, who perhaps find me to be intimidating or already too deep in my spiritual quest. The latter category disappoints and confuses me. As deep as I choose to delve into myself, and how open I can be about that process with others, I am quite sensitive; you cannot open yourself without exposing yourself as well. It raises even more questions: Should I tone it down so I can be more readily accepted? Is acceptance from others what I'm seeking? If I were more spiritually aligned, at peace internally, I would not be seeking approval or validation from others. However,

I am on this earth, and it does get a bit lonely at times. I feel lost, and that is when the pain seeps out. Then I have to dig deep, restore my soul, feel its journey, and be in touch with my purpose.

Meeting people who are in alignment with their path is a glorious thing. It seems that everything opens up for them because it is supposed to be. A favorite powerful quote from the late Dr. Wayne Dyer describes this phenomenon: "There are no such things as coincidences, just universal timing." I would add be open; do not be attached to the outcome. Only then will you see what is supposed to be for you.

I have learned on my journey that I can be intentional about my needs and that I may be too focused on them appearing in one form only. When what I want shows up in a different, unexpected way, I have to remain open; otherwise I might miss it. I have learned to open myself up to opportunities.

I become that which I give my attention. When I paid attention to the negative, it manifested in health issues and a negative state of mind. Science supports this notion. Part of the midbrain is called the limbic system, and from here our emotions originate. The limbic system acts as a filter for our external experiences and works in tandem with the front part of our brain, the frontal lobes or frontal cortex. The frontal cortex interprets external events and communicates with the limbic system, which then produces the appropriate emotion. If the limbic system is in a normal, cool state, it will interpret the external events as positive and we will have positive thoughts and a sense of well-being. When the limbic system is overactive, the negative filter is on, interpreting external events as negative. Automatic negative thoughts (ANT) describe the results of some people's overactive limbic system.

Conversely, the flipside is also true: we can actually change the makeup of our brain by how we think. Our thoughts have extraordinary power! This possibility is not realized to its full potential. If it were so simple, why wouldn't we just think positively to fix things, to make ourselves better when we feel ill, to cure ourselves of any ailments? I often ask these questions myself, and of course there is no obvious answer.

My spiritual journey has had so many twists and turns along the way, I could never adequately describe all of them. Along with the many high points of my spiritual journey, battling with depression continued, as did feelings of inferiority. What was behind this? I started to wonder if science could help shed more light on these things. After all, the mind and the spirit are connected; maybe we just need to see where our research leads us? I came to realize that this quest is indeed a major source of purpose for my life.

I'm curious to see how we can use science to provide strong evidence for this "spiritual hypothesis" that so fascinates me. How can we increase our level of consciousness to our higher selves? How can we train the brain to make us more aware and enlightened through meditation and prayer? How can we alter our neuronal pathways to accommodate a more positive conscious mind? Can we alleviate unnecessary internal suffering by having a positive mind? Alternatively, can we become more spiritual if we alter the brain? My next chapter will explore these questions, the scientific side of spirituality, and much more.

PART III

THE SCIENTIFIC

As a neuroscientist, I was curious to see if any compelling scientific evidence supports the powerful connection between spiritual practices and our well-being, or whether any physiological neuronal pathways are associated with people's spirituality. I was delighted though not surprised to discover there is indeed some evidence for both. Neurologists, psychiatrists, and cognitive neuroscientists have been asking similar questions in their quest to determine how spiritual practices like mindfulness meditation can be leveraged to help people with neurological and psychological disorders.

Advancements in medical technologies help us understand the mechanisms underlying neurological and psychological disorders, as well as spiritual experiences. Neuroimaging provides visual evidence of neuronal activity in the brain, and has been instrumental in turning the tide for people suffering with neurological or psychological disorders. In centuries past, these people were considered to be possessed, but now we understand that their illness is treatable through medication and modulation.

As we discussed in the introduction, these are the sorts of advances that tend to paint spirituality as primitive and waiting to be supplanted by science; the logic states that the spiritual practices of yesterday will be replaced by the medicinal treatments of today. That's not the whole story though, or even most of it. Spirituality and neuroscience are not mutually exclusive fields of thought for treating ailments like depression, and advancements in science can actually help us better understand spirituality, as opposed to replacing it.

In this chapter, I will explore these advancements and how they are helping to develop a deeper understanding of such disorders, and the role spiritual practices may play in enhancing or complementing such treatments. I will frame this discussion through my own experience, sharing my interest in neurological disorders (mainly depression) and exploring the reported benefits of integrating nonconventional spiritual practices like mindfulness meditation. It's important to highlight that the intent of this chapter is not to convince you spiritual mindfulness practices can or should replace traditional medical treatment such as medication for the disorders I will discuss. To reiterate, it's to share how mindfulness practices has helped me reach a place of emotional well being and the emerging science which support what I instinctively know to be true about the benefits of adopting such practices in my life.

It's also important to know how we reached a reasonable level of understanding about the mechanisms underlying neurological and psychological disorders before exploring the potential of validating the effects that spirituality may have on the brain. My interest in the brain and its functionalities began in the lecture theaters at the University of East London, where I was introduced to the world of neurophysiology and psychopharmacology. I found myself intrigued by the physiological mechanisms behind psychosomatic and movement disorders like Parkinson's Disease (PD), Alzheimer's, depression, and Huntington's Disease. These disorders of the mind have been around for centuries, during which most people suffering from them were tragically misunderstood, misdiagnosed, and mistreated, often shunned by society and treated as outcasts.

At the end of the Middle Ages, women with certain movement and psychiatric disorders like epilepsy, Huntington's, chorea, and hysteria, whose symptoms might include abnormal body movements, tremors, and convulsions, were often considered to be witches or possessed by the devil. They were readily blamed for the world's ills and often condemned to die by burning at the stake. This practice became a craze in many countries, particularly in Northern Europe, through the late eighteenth century. With advancements in medicine, however, doctors better understood these disorders, and they were reclassified as illnesses.

In the 1940s and 1950s, controversial psychosurgery was used indiscriminately to treat severe depression, anxiety, obsessional thoughts, and self-injurious behavior. During this era medication wasn't available for such disorders and typically people suffering were confined to asylums. When psychosurgery came around it was initially seen as a godsend, since when carefully performed on select patients it relieved suffering. Unlike today, there were no regulations, Institutional Review Board (IRB), or clinical studies being conducted on this form of treatment. Inevitably, there were reported cases of early, misguided application of prefrontal and transorbital lobotomies (often by psychiatrists in their offices with a pickax and no anesthesia). In such cases this irreversible procedure resulted in significant negative outcomes, including personality changes, loss of executive function, and cognitive decline. Even though in selected cases the treatment produced good outcome, the overshadowing poor results from misguided application of the treatment, coupled with the rising availability of psychiatric medications thankfully led to the demise of such psychosurgery in the late twentieth century.

It's amazing that the brain withstood the invasion and, indeed, that any patients survived the ordeal. Equally amazing is that, though there were some select cases of success, the unregulated practice of lobotomies was considered acceptable medical treatment. Evidence-based medical therapy is now the first approach for psychotherapy such as depression; however this is not universally available and there are no true guidelines for matching the patient to the optimal treatment. This ultimately means it is the physician's and patient's choice on the type of therapy they receive. If patients don't respond well, electrical stimulation techniques like electroconvulsive therapy (ECT) may be used to treat patients. If they don't respond well to this noninvasive form of stimulation, psychosurgery may be considered as an alternative treatment. Medical technology has evolved from the ablative psychosurgery of old to a more contemporary neuromodulation, a less invasive and more precise form of psychosurgery and brain modulation through electrical impulse, which has no intent to damage. These treatments are heavily regulated, and require extensive clinical evidence prior to approval. Once approved, each case is very specific to the disease state, the symptoms to be treated, and the area to be stimulated. Such rigor is certainly warranted to ensure that people will not experience inappropriate "shock" treatments such as depicted in the vein of the classic novel *One Flew Over the Cuckoo's Nest.*

Even though we have come a long way in understanding psychiatric and movement disorders, people with such disorders, especially dystonia, Tourette syndrome, or Obsessive Compulsive Disorder (OCD) may still be shunned by society or may hide themselves away. Some with severe symptoms are kept in psychiatric facilities and treated with psychiatric drugs. Fortunately, as we gain further insights into these disorders of the brain, we are able to care more appropriately for people suffering in this manner. We still have much to learn before we can easily and consistently diagnose patients with psychiatric disorders and apply appropriate treatments that have consistently good clinical outcomes.

While movement disorders are often idiopathic—their specific cause unknown—most stem from dysfunctional neuronal pathways in deep structures of the brain called the basal ganglia. The basal ganglia have to function well in order for the motor cortex, an area higher up in the brain responsible for movement, to work well. The two are interconnected. Research in these areas of the brain has led to the development of proven therapies that successfully treat the symptoms of some of the disorders in carefully selected patients, improving their quality of life as well as that of their caregivers.

Movement disorders like Parkinson's have become easier to diagnose because of established tests or rating scales used to assess major symptoms like tremor, bradykinesia, and rigidity. However, treatment options and their efficacy vary around the world, the result of a multitude of factors like correct diagnosis, the patient's willingness to undergo certain treatments, and in the case of neuromodulation the precise location of electrodes in the desired anatomical target. The frequent overlap between movement and psychiatric disorders further complicates matters. One typically exacerbates the other, as commonly seen in depressed Parkinson's patients with tremor. The tremor may be amplified by anxiety, and dystonia is typically induced in patients treated for psychosis with neuroleptics. The combined presentation of such symptoms often presents challenges in determining underlying causes; hence, the search for improved treatments is ongoing.

In another example, treatment of the neurological disorder epilepsy has progressed with the advancement of medical technologies. Scientists now have the ability to physiologically monitor, detect, and record seizures in epileptic patients. Taking these assessments one step further, closed-loop systems can react to correct certain physiological measurements or keep them within defined parameters. Research is underway to establish a consistent, reliable means of using a closed-loop system to predict the event of a seizure and prevent it from occurring. Closed-loop models are also being used to discover physiological biomarkers either to reliably detect or to monitor the progression of Parkinson's, an understanding of which would significantly advance treatment options for patients.

These instances are cases of medical technology helping us understand the physical mechanisms of conditions humanity previously found mystifying. We use these advances to diagnose conditions and treat symptoms before they occur, all because when modern scientists look at the brain, we now know better than ever before what we're looking at. It's not a reach to ask, then: how can we leverage these same advances, these same technologies, to help us understand the neuroscience behind spirituality?

Thanks to these advancing medical technologies, we now not only can treat these neurological disorders, but we also have the tools to provide evidence to support what we have known for centuries about the power of the unconscious brain. In the twentieth century Sigmund Freud developed well-known theories of the unconscious mind–using an iceberg to describe three main states of mind. The tip of the iceberg is the conscious mind, consisting of thoughts focused on the present. The middle of the iceberg is the preconscious mind, which consists of thoughts retrieved from memory–which I believe contributes to what I call the "chatter." Lastly, the bottom of the iceberg, which is significant and unseen, is the unconscious mind, where the important processes that govern our behavior lie.

The unconscious mind, the unseen layer of the iceberg, is worth exploring here. It's thought to be mediated by the preconscious and conscious mind (which I will now collectively call the conscious mind). Still, today a popular school of thought maintains that sensory inputs in the unconscious brain play an important role in our conscious brain through integrated circuits, which help to create a full picture of the world. Whilst Freud's theories were very well adopted and understood, they weren't considered highly scientific, as it was impossible to test or measure the unconscious mind during that time. With the advancements in medical technologies and procedures in our present era, some evidence is now emerging. For example, a Massachusetts Institute of Technology (MIT) study on patients under anesthesia provided physiological evidence of the brain's ability to receive information when unconscious. The authors suggest the information received when unconscious is not integrated into the conscious brain, which ultimately limits our ability to see the "full picture of the world." We need both the conscious and unconscious brain; however, the conscious brain appears to dominate.

The conscious brain is active, constantly busy creating our thoughts, feelings, and emotions and housing our memories. As a result, our minds are full of chatter, and through practices like meditation we aim to quiet our thoughts and tap into the silence of the unconscious brain in order to create a sense of peace and well-being. This makes me wonder if we can leverage the well-documented power of the unconscious brain to advance medical treatments, promote healing, and become more fully integrated (by tapping more into the unconscious brain and/or by increasing sensory inputs into the conscious brain) through nontraditional practices like meditation. This would represent a flip from the paradigm outlined earlier: rather than medical advancement making us rethink our spiritual practices, here, the activity within our unconscious brains would have us reexamining the way in which we study our brains.

A natural place to start examining how we interact with our unconscious minds is meditation. Meditation, the act of parsing through all the clutter in our minds such that we can actually be present and hear our internal self, is already linked to treating emotional health. I'm grateful for it as I personally benefit from the effect meditation can have on my emotional well-being.

Approximately 5 percent of the global population suffers from some form of depression, from minor depression like dysthymia to severe, long-lasting major depressive disorders, to the most severe but less common psychotic depression. Indeed, the World Health Organization considers it to be a worldwide epidemic. No matter the form, whether reactive to a stressful situation or event, clinical due to chemical imbalance, or triggered by or coexisting as part of an illness, depression is indiscriminate and can impact anyone at any time in their life.

Many suffering from depression do so in silence. The stigma associated with depression lends a reluctance to reveal the vulnerability and pain it brings. For many years I skillfully managed and masked my depression. I didn't want the world to see that, despite my appearance of being strong, smart, and together, I harbored many negative thoughts about myself. I suffered in silence. As my pain increased, so did my determination to seek spiritual solace. I evolved rapidly. The more comfortable I became with my truth, the more open I became to seeking help and talking openly about my truth. Accepting what is and sharing my feelings with those I trust is a relief.

Often we resist acknowledging the truth and, more importantly, we resist seeking support. Realizing we are not alone, that others share our experience, is comforting. Learning about different ways in which one can be supported is not only comforting but also impactful. A simple but effective way of receiving support is by seeing a therapist or psychologist on a regular basis. In this safe place, you openly discuss your feelings and receive support, be it cognitive, medical, or both, from a specialist. While there is also a stigma attached to seeing a therapist, especially in certain cultures, intervention, particularly at an early stage, can prevent certain forms of depression from bringing you unnecessarily to an all-time low.

When I'm in a tough spot or I feel myself slipping into a place of negativity, I have trained myself to unconsciously and spontaneously counter my negative chatter with reality-check questions and positive thoughts. I've learned to stop resisting being present, and I've learned to love—or at least accept—what is. With this practice, honed over many years, my spirit is miraculously uplifted enough for me to get on with my day with a light heart, an open mind, and a smile on my face. Meditation and prayer are key practices that help me achieve this more positive and peaceful state of mind. The reason is simple: meditation is perhaps the best practice currently available to us for accessing our unconscious minds. If so much of our well-being is tied to the state of this space in our brains, and a spiritual practice like meditation is the best method for reaching into it ourselves, shouldn't we be exploring how better to do this? If so, why should we be concerned whether meditation is considered spiritual or medical? My hope is if I stay the course with my mindfulness practices, I will continue to evolve spiritually and arrive at a meditative state of being, as opposed to being a person who occasionally practices meditation. A vision I have for my life, it's not just a hobby. This, I think, is my ultimate goal and perhaps my purpose for this lifetime.

Through conversations with friends and like-minded people, I've learned about the power of being still and meditating when my depressed moods are prominent. Being still, even if only for a moment, is healing. It allows me to be present and to connect with the energy the universe readily emits. During meditation, I concentrate on tapping into the silence between my thoughts, which calms them, grounds me, and brings me to a place of inner peace. I practice meditation with the belief that I'll be more in tune with my instincts and my spiritual guides and thus make better decisions or take better actions in alignment with my spiritual purpose.

I try to practice meditation every morning for a few minutes. After years of exploring different techniques, I can now find that peaceful place in seconds, wherever I am, be it on a plane, in my office, or in a crowded room. It's like anchoring in sports, when a player is about to take what could be the winning kick, the world is watching, and he or she has to zone out to a place of grounding to do what's expected amid the chaos and excitement, knowing this kick could mean winning it all for the team. In meditation, this same anchoring action brings one to a place of peace to make the right decision, whether under stress or not.

It took a while before I got to this place. Once I understood the mechanism behind meditation, the process became easier.

The best time for me to do a long meditation is following exercise, after I have been concentrating on running, rowing, or cycling for thirty minutes or so. It takes work to meditate: the action is mindful as you silence your thoughts and tune in to your other senses.

If your mood is depressed, it's hard to move to a place of inner peace. The very nature of a depressed mood means you don't have the motivation to do anything other than sit in the pain and willfully disconnect from the outside world. Through meditation, thinking positive thoughts can bring the desired inner peace and a willingness to reconnect with the world. I've experienced this peace several times though my practice. This work is ongoing: the negative thoughts still occur, but less frequently and for shorter periods.

Part of the healing process as I mentioned earlier is sharing this experience openly with others. The stigma attached to depression or depressed moods can only be erased when people realize how prevalent this experience is and how preventative measures such as therapy and mindfulness meditation can help manage the situation. Mindfulness meditation is growing in popularity as a means to calm the mind and reduce stress, depression, and anxiety. It can be used to promote emotional stability and has been incorporated into medical practice to prevent relapses in people recovering from depression. It's used to help focus on the now, the moment-to-moment thoughts, and not the narrative or negative chatter—the constant replay of negative experiences, expectations or feelings.

When I think about the times I experience negative chatter, which can rapidly lead to a downward spiral, I realize my chatter is based on negative experiences in the past and not the reality of now. I have a tendency to hang on to the narrative as if it's a permanent, inflexible aspect that governs my life. I feed this narrative with false presumptions or fear. However, when I counter my negative thoughts with reality-check questions, my truthful answers help me realize that while the narrative may have been true in the past, it does not necessarily apply to my current experience.

The root of most negative thoughts is FEAR: False Expectations Are Real or False Evidence Appearing Real. Both are based on perception and not reality; in our minds, however, our perception is our reality. When we recognize danger and react appropriately, fear is warranted as the body physiologically prepares for flight or fight. Our ability to assess a bad situation is necessary to keep ourselves safe and is the real purpose of fear. When FEAR unnecessarily dominates, it's unhealthy, emotionally attacking our minds in a negative way. Meditation can indirectly help to control fear by reducing levels of anxiety and stress. One core component in successful meditation practices is belief that the nonconventional practice of silencing our thoughts and re-channeling our energy will yield positive outcomes. Adding to this belief, advancement of medical technologies has helped to provide scientific evidence to support the power of meditation on our sense of well-being.

As a neuroscientist, I understand that the process of mindfulness meditation has some physiological basis. A quick Internet search reveals clinical studies that have used advanced technologies like neuroimaging to explore pathways associated with this practice. Functional magnetic resonance imaging (fMRI) is used to measure metabolic activity in the brain, showing increase or decrease in blood flow. In people who practice mindfulness meditation, select fMRI studies have shown an increased blood flow to the prefrontal cortex; other studies have shown a reduction in amygdala size. The amygdala is the part of the limbic system directly involved in the emotional processing of both positive and negative stimuli. It's directly involved in our sense of well-being, survival instinct, memory and fear conditioning. Mindfulness meditation has been shown to lower the amygdala's response to emotional stimuli, which may contribute to increasing our sense of well-being.

This visual evidence provides proof of what practitioners of these alternative techniques have long suspected. Meditation can bring a variety of spiritual experiences that are associated with activity in neuronal networks linked to the prefrontal cortex and amygdala. Also shown is an increase in recall memory in some subjects, and meditation is increasingly being integrated into medical-treatment pathways for chronic illnesses like cancer to help alleviate pain and manage the patient's sense of well-being.

The concept of training the brain through mindfulness meditation—a process that has yielded positive results for me—is the foundation of mindfulness-based cognitive therapy (MBCT), primarily used as a preventative measure for patients with a history of depression. As they access their present-moment pathway through focused meditation, this pathway is strengthened, while the pathway related to negative thoughts is weakened. Most who practice mindfulness meditation believe the primary outcome is inner peace, tranquility, and sometimes transcendence—being more open to spiritual beliefs and practices.

Many studies provide additional empirical confirmation that meditation and alternative modalities affect not just mood but the brain itself. Researchers and thought leaders have conducted studies using neuroimaging to identify neuronal pathways associated with emotional changes, or regulation associated with mindfulness training (MT).

One of these thought leaders is the distinguished Professor of Psychology Zindel Segal, know for combining mindfulness meditation with evidence-based cognitive behavioral therapy (Mindfulness-based cognitive therapy: MBCT). His technique was inspired by the world-renowned Dr. Jon Kabat-Zinn's mindfulness-based stress-reduction program (MBSR), which integrates the holistic approach of using both body and mind to heal physical and psychological symptoms. Zingel Segal was the primary collaborator with leading thought leaders, including Professors Sid Kennedy and Helen Mayberg from University of Toronto and Emory respectively. Also included were Associate Professors at the University of Toronto Norman Farb and Adam Anderson, whose mindfulness studies have been pivotal in increasing our understanding of the mechanisms behind mindfulness meditation. The group has built on work that hypothesized about processes associated with identifying with the self, and interacting with stimuli outside of one's self. Zingel Segal and collaborators pioneered Cognitive Behavioral Therapy (CBT) research for depression. Through further research, specifically in 2007 and 2010, Farb, Segal *et al* reported on a couple of fascinating studies that identified a default circuit in the brain called the medial prefrontal cortex (mPFC), which is associated with our states of awareness. Using positron emission tomography (PET) scans and fMRI, they showed that mindfulness training suppressed the activity of one pathway and increased the activity on another within this circuit. These pathways are associated with the two different states of awareness, one with moment-to-moment thoughts (being present) and one with thoughts linked to experience over time, the negative chatter (narrative).

In experienced mindfulness-meditation subjects, the study showed a marked decrease in mPFC activity (chatter) and an increased engagement in structures on the right lateral side, the insula, secondary somatosensory cortex, and the inferior parietal lobe. In other words, in a typical state when the mind is unable to distinguish chatter from the present moment, mindfulness meditation helps us to increase our present-moment thoughts by activating a pathway in a higher center in the brain.

This work is exciting because it strongly suggests that training the brain to suppress negative chatter can alter our neuronal pathways to help us think positively, which in turn suggests we can train our brain to enhance our sense of well-being. This theory aligns with neuronal plasticity research I conducted for my PhD. My work examined the adult brain's ability to alter functional pathways by changing our experience innocuously. My findings provided further evidence that the adult brain is not hardwired and is indeed plastic. This plasticity allows us to be more in tune with our unconscious brain through meditative practices.

Plasticity can be explained by the Hebbian theory of synapses. The space between two neurons that are activated both chemically and electrically allows them to connect with each other, passing information from one to the next along the neuronal pathway. These synaptic connections are strengthened or weakened through our experience. If we regularly use a certain neuronal pathway, we strengthen its connections. If we don't use the pathway, we can weaken these neuronal connections. Thus, the brain is plastic: it can go from having strong pathways to weak pathways based on usage.

The study performed in Toronto used fMRI to identify pathways associated with both states of self-awareness—the positive/moment and negative/narrative—and showed that these pathways can be modulated through meditation.

As I was working on this book, the universe opened up and presented me with many wonderful opportunities, one of which was to meet one of the collaborators on the study, Professor Helen Mayberg. Professor Mayberg has deep experience and interest in brain networks connected to depression, and is involved in many studies using neuronal imaging and neurophysiological techniques in her quest to understand all treatments. Soon after I had finished reading publications on mindfulness training and depression, I was scheduled to visit Emory for work. I asked a colleague to connect us, and to my pleasant surprise Professor Mayberg quickly responded to my e-mail and was gracious enough to meet with me during my visit. I had lots of questions for her.

When I arrived at Emory University, I was concerned about how our conversation would go. I didn't want her to think I was strange, and I had to make clear that my interest in meeting her was personal and not Medtronic business. We talked for more than an hour and a half, beyond the time she had offered me. She was delightful—open and interested in why I wanted to meet with her. Excited and nervous, I quickly explained a tiny bit about my path and the book, outlining the questions I still had and why I wanted to speak to her.

She explained that her research group had not yet explored the topic as thoroughly as they wished, and they still had a ton of questions about mindfulness training and the processes in our brain and how meditation affects us. She opened up to me, exploring depths where she doesn't normally go. I soaked it all in. She talked about expanding our level of consciousness and how mindfulness training helps us to do this. She explained it simply: when you are sick with severe depression, you are disassociated with anything outside of yourself, the external world. You are not connected, and you can't be because the main pathway associated with connection outside of one's self is "chattered," which in turn disables you as a person. You become nonfunctional. The disengagement may be due to mistiming of the neurons connecting with each other in the neuronal pathways in the mPFC. Her research explores how to switch the pathways back to being synchronized so you can reconnect with the outside environment. Once someone is re-engaged, mindfulness training can help increase periods of positive thoughts, one's connectivity with the external and the present, as opposed to internal negative thoughts. She described it as a continuum from sick patients to those who have negative moods. Sick patients lack the ability to switch off the brake, to return to synchronicity.

An important point—one I hadn't considered previously—is that with depression, the brain is characterized by the disconnection of certain neuronal pathways, rather than its damage. Damage or atrophy in for example the frontal cortex or hippocampus means that connections in neuronal pathways are mistimed, which affects how information is transferred, which ultimately affects the way one relates with the external world. When we are off, we can become disconnected from the outside world. However, this disconnection is reversible and modulation can improve communication between neurons and help us reconnect to the world. Mindfulness training can play a role in helping the brain remain connected once the timing issue is resolved. "Releasing the brakes" can get patients unstuck, and then they can shift to the normal state of flux between positive and negative thoughts. Patients get to a state where they can choose if they want to be mindful or not. Mindfulness training can help expand their capacity for positive thoughts and their ability to let the negative thoughts go by.

Professor Mayberg went on to explain that the typical normal state of our brains is a survival mode. The brain has to remember the negative experiences so it can prevent them from happening again. This is called "plasticity for the negative": we remember even the smallest of negative experiences and not so much the small positive ones. She and I never discussed it, but I'm sure fear comes into play here as well; it's part of the survival process. Patients sick with depression lose their ability to shift in and out of negative thoughts. Instead, those negative thoughts consume all their brain's energy and can't be switched off. Drug therapy or modulation can help them move out of the negative loop, after which mindfulness training is impactful. Patients develop a process or method to prevent slipping back into the negative spiral or disengaging with the external environment.

In the course of our conversation, for the first time I realized I was maybe a person experiencing intense negative moods as opposed to depressed moods, which I've learned to successfully manage. It takes work, but now when I slip, a spirit or instinct picks me up and makes me do what I know will make a difference: exercise and mindfulness training. Professor Mayberg also talked about shifting our zero, or baseline. When someone is sick, they don't want to or are unable to function. When a person is well, the baseline shifts in and out of negative states. Typically, one doesn't remember that previous experience; the present experience becomes the new zero, and the reaction to it depends on the individual. For example, you may become connected to the outside world and not like what you see or what you have done, and this view can shift you into a negative mood. Shifting your zero can occur in many ways and this depends on the type of depression. Major depressive disorders may involve some form of modulation in order for the patient to reconnect with the external world. Milder forms of depression may require medication, but mindfulness meditation training can play a role here as well.

I brought up the idea that creativity and spiritual growth come from emotional pain, getting at one of my original questions: why do our souls need the human experience for evolution, and why does the experience have to be so painful? Professor Mayberg made another point I had never considered: the evolution or creation comes if you survive the emotional pain. She posed a question: what is taking place or what process is formed in the brain as a result of the emotionally painful experience? Whatever it is, it helps us survive. Our emotional experiences have the power to shape us on a biological level: positive experiences can shape our minds and behaviors in ways that benefit us, while negative moments, times of emotional trauma, can have equal and possibly irreversible effects on who we are if left unaddressed. Out of our brains' responses to these experiences, creativity may evolve or perhaps enhance itself. I remain fascinated by her thoughts and wonder if, under these circumstances, a creativity pathway between the conscious and unconscious brain is being formed.

Despite our advancements in medical technology, there is of course so much we still don't know. However, I'm optimistic it's just a matter of time before we have a deeper understanding of the disorders of the mind and how spiritual practices can affect our thinking. I'm grateful Professor Mayberg and her teams are exploring such unknowns in a credible, thoroughly scientific way. Her brilliance and openness in seeking holistic approaches for her patients with depression can only help to bring treatments for such disorders to the next frontier.

Depression is challenging to understand and manage. First and foremost, it is not even a unified concept; it can appear in many forms for a variety of reasons, which means that research and unifying hypotheses can be difficult to construct. In order to make progress, a testable hypothesis first needs to be identified. Depression, in its many forms, involves several physiological, emotional, and external factors. Physiological neurotransmitters, or hormones, play a role. An imbalance of hormones may help to either suppress or engage activities of the relevant parts of the brain. Traditionally, depression is treated with antidepressants like the popular serotonin reuptake inhibitors (SSRIs), which rebalance the hormones. Some believe the release of endorphins—a type of hormone—through frequent exercise helps to suppress negative thoughts. Exercise is one of the strategies I use to lift my mood. I feel euphoric after a long session, and when I meditate immediately afterward I experience the most powerful effects of that practice.

Because endorphins are natural analgesics, they trigger positive feelings when released in response to neurotransmitters through exercise and meditation. Endorphins interact with pain and mood circuits in the brain, reducing the perception of pain. Meditation has been shown to alleviate both pain and depression, both physical and emotional duress.

Pain, the place where all these concepts of spirituality and neuroscience most frequently converge. Pain is the reason we go seeking for answers; we would not explore treatment if we were not hurting. It's a central motif of my journey, as it is for all of us. I sought new forms of spirituality because, in varying ways throughout my life, I was in emotional pain. It's why I turn to my spirit guides, and have a need to soothe my mind through mindful practices like meditation. It's also why I believe it's critical we treat spirituality and neuroscience as complementary. These are not theoretical problems we are trying to solve; we are actually trying to find practices that make us feel better and maintain good emotional health.

Pain is subjective, and is a very complex field to explore and understand. Similar to the disorders discussed earlier in this chapter, this complex phenomenon is influenced by multiple factors. Pain is unique. It cannot be seen, touched, or measured objectively, but it's real, and everyone will experience pain at some point in their lives. There are varying degrees of acute and chronic pain with known causes, such as an injury. There are also many incidences where the cause of pain is unknown. Chronic pain and depression often coexist. Chronic pain can lead to a plethora of issues like anxiety and depression, while depression can cause pain such as headaches and backaches.

Antidepressant medications may relieve both depression and pain. As mentioned earlier, spiritual practices like mindfulness meditation have been shown to suppress depression as well as pain. Some forms of chronic pain can also be alleviated by modulation, or even by the way we think. Having a positive attitude or engaging in distracting thoughts can alleviate discomfort for some people. Since everyone's experience is different, many options for pain management exist: analgesics, noninvasive forms of stimulation (transcutaneous electrical nerve stimulation, or TENS), or surgical intervention like intrathecal drug delivery (morphine being delivered directly to the spinal cord) or spinal cord stimulation.

When I experience pain after a surgery or during an illness, I try to manage it with traditional analgesics. I have noticed that during the period of suffering and recovery I tend to be more spirituality aware, questioning my path and purpose while seeking comfort from more focused prayer and meditation. When the pain subsides and I have healed from my illness, I feel more spiritually evolved and connected with the universe. My awareness of the things that matter the most to me is heightened, and I'm able to be present in the moment.

Meditation, which has also worked for me, has been reported to temporarily alleviate chronic pain in some patients. It may be viewed as a distractive approach or as a method to override pain perception psychologically. I am reminded of Ronald Melzack and Patrick Wall's gate-control theory of pain (1965). As an undergrad in London I was fortunate to attend a lecture by Dr. Wall. He used an example of a horse finishing a race with a broken leg to explain how the brain can override some pain signals by producing endorphins. The gate-control theory of pain is widely used to describe the physiological and psychological influences of pain. The theory takes into account the effects of emotion and thoughts on pain perception, hypothesizing that within the elegantly complex pain system "nerve gates" play a key role in regulating pain signals that reach the brain—and that these gates can be influenced by sensory, emotional, and cognitive factors. The emotional component of this theory may explain why meditation and distractive approaches can sometimes provide relief from pain. Meditation stimulates the release of endorphins, according to some studies.

When I think about phantom-limb pain (pain in the area of an amputated limb where the tissue at the stump site has healed), I'm fascinated by how readily and quickly it seems the brain is able to reorganize pathways to other areas in response to an amputation. There are many theories that try to explain why phantom pain exists. I believe that the matrix of connections between neuronal pathways in the somatosensory cortex is vast, and that there is very apparent overlap among pathways associated with pain, neurological and psychological disorders, and possibly spiritual thinking. Therefore, I wonder if specific areas in the brain are directly associated with spirituality or self-transcendence (a personality trait used to measure one's predisposition to spirituality).

A study conducted in Udine, Italy, suggests this very thing. Cognitive neuroscientist Cosimo Urgesi and his colleagues at Udine University studied patients with brain tumors to assess their level of self-transcendence before and after surgery. Self-transcendence, or a person's ability to overcome the limits of his or her own self, is a concept often linked to spirituality; in order to conceive of things within us that we cannot ordinarily access, we must first learn how to get beyond those self-imposed limits. These patients reported increased levels of self-transcendence in patients with selective damage (brain tumors) to the inferior posterior parietal lobes and the right angular gyrus. These areas at the back of the brain are involved in how we perceive our bodies in spatial relation to the external world. Patients with selective damage in the frontal temporal cortex showed no change or a slight decrease in their self-transcendence levels.

While these findings differ from the neuroimaging studies, the investigators interpreted their findings as a hint of evidence of the role the posterior brain plays in determining self-transcendence or spiritual awareness. They suggest their findings "cast new light on the neurobiological bases of altered spiritual and religious attitudes and behaviors in neurological mental disorders." While this study is open to methodological improvement for measuring self-transcendence, it's a decent pioneering close-up look at spirituality.

I'm encouraged by the possibilities these startling outcomes imply, that spiritual thinking arises from specific areas of the brain. Coupled with the groundbreaking neuroimaging work of Segal, his collaborators, and other thought leaders in this field, we are gaining much deeper insights and increased understanding of the effects spirituality has on the brain. It's not just a complex phenomenon we can feel and interpret; it's a phenomenon with scientific evidence to support its existence.

This is not to say we need science to prove what we instinctively know to be true about spirituality. But research or scientific proof combined with proven efficacy are crucial requirements so that new therapies can receive approval for use as treatment. Hence, credible scientific evidence to support noninvasive unconventional approaches like meditation can only help to integrate these practices into more traditional treatment pathways to enhance our therapies, bringing them to the next level of efficacy.

In thinking about what it would take to achieve full integration, I wonder whether translating the effects of the spiritual into a technological clinical application (or therapy) will transform our current approaches. For example, neural prosthesis brain-machine interfaces in paralyzed patients have been shown to leverage thoughts to control machines or move computer cursors using only brain waves to select letters on a keyboard. Brain chips are being studied for memory repair and to mimic neuronal networks. Behind all of this is the power of belief, which may be evoked by the modulation of certain pathways in the posterior part of the brain. While this kind of thinking may seem quite "out of the box," I'm convinced it's the direction we must explore to unlock the brain's full potential.

Answering such questions will either allow us to leverage our full powers to manage and even overcome neurodegenerative and emotional disorders or push us toward a different therapeutic path. Either way, we will be making progress.

PART IV

THE CONVERGENCE

To some, a connection between our emotional sense of well-being and our physical health feels like a stretch. This is often because the link doesn't seem quite intuitive to people who don't feel comfortable with spirituality as a concept. There is one school of thought that supports the notion that our physical being is entirely separate from our emotions, thoughts, and feelings. The idea of spending time tending to our emotions is sometimes deemed a luxury. It may seem easier to bury emotions and push through life. Just pull your socks up, or suck it up. During my stressful experience I didn't have the time to spend on tending to my emotions. I had too many pressing barriers to overcome and it seemed like an out-of-reach luxury, only for the privileged few who could afford the time and the expense. Therefore I was one of those who believed in pulling my socks up and getting on with it.

An alternative emerging school of thought discussed in depth in my previous chapter is that spirituality can be *directly* tied to our physical selves, by way of the makeup of our brains. Believing this is not a matter of speculation, rather one with scientific grounding. A challenge however comes with this school of thought when starting from a position that spirituality is the solution before considering the root cause of the issue. So let's reframe the issue around the ailments, the things that have us seeking solutions (either scientific or spiritual) in the first place.

Take stress. Far more than just "feeling overwhelmed," stress is becoming increasingly understood to have very real physical ramifications, and is much more of a physiological problem as opposed to an anecdotally emotional one. It's directly tied to our body chemistry: when we are stressed, our adrenal glands produce hormones like cortisol, which help us execute a fight or flight response more efficiently in threatening situations. When we get stressed, these chemical messengers send a signal to our brains to shut down non-essential functions, so as to focus on survival. Unfortunately, the same hormones are released regardless of what's stressing us out; whether we're being chased by a wild animal or preparing to give a presentation, our body chemistry is going to react the same. Hence physical reactions like getting "choked up" or feeling "butterflies" or even losing control of our bowels all become possibilities, even when they're detrimental to us living our lives. The physical symptoms can be wide-ranging, and all stem from what is originally thought of as a "feeling."

More importantly though, stress occurs as a response to our life experiences. It's tied to how we live, and how we feel about the way we're living, even if we don't initially realize it. Looking back at my own life, I am convinced that for my first two decades, I was experiencing chronic stress, stemming from continual and intense emotional pressure. From my childhood experience, my young brother passing away and my rigorous academic journey that was an emotional roller coaster rife with racial and intellectual challenges as well as moments of pure jubilation. I don't remember feeling any sense of peace during my younger years and early academic career. However, this shaped me; it had me retreating inside myself, and became the driving force behind much of my spiritual questioning. As described earlier, I literally had a breakdown, ending up in the hospital at the moment my mind and body burned out, tired from the constant fighting. My emotional health had been ignored, which triggered a chemical response in my brain, which over the course of nearly eighteen years culminated in severe physical debilitation. Funny enough, while recuperating from my breakdown only my physical body was being treated. My emotional state of well-being was not even acknowledged or discussed even though now it's obvious this was probably the root of my physical aliment.

Put this way, I'm hoping the link between our emotions, brain chemistry, and physical being makes it easier to understand why someone in my position would seek solutions to treat both the physical symptoms and emotional responses to my actual life experiences. In other words, it might become a more acceptable and sought-after practice for people to manage their inner selves as a means of also taking care of their physical health.

An "inner self." To the spiritual this could mean a soul that requires recognition and constant nurturing to support the evolution of one's spiritual self, or to the stringently scientific-minded people this could refer only to brain chemistry. "Brain chemistry," even to a neurophysiologist like me, starts to feel somewhat faceless and inhuman when we consider ailments and imbalances with real, widespread, and severe human effects, like depression. As we're starting to understand, depression also represents a space in which we're finding more credible evidence that spiritual practice and brain chemistry might not be so separate after all.

For far too long depression and other psychological disorders have been misdiagnosed. Depressed people were often thought of as "being too sad," or "negative" in response to experiences that either they or others found to be "incorrect" or "too much." This view has long been deemed incomplete as we learn more about the brain, however, it does speak to a very basic and interesting instinct: the way we emotionally feel has long been tied to our life experiences. It's a very obvious thing to point out, and as neuroscientists who study depression would say, it's very incomplete; but it is a basic point worth coming back to in a moment.

We now know that certain forms of depression are the result of chemical imbalances in the brain. When certain pathways are blocked or disrupted, and certain neurotransmitter levels are thus altered, depression, anxiety, and other ailments can occur and present itself in a variety of symptoms. Usually these neurotransmitters are dopamine, norepinephrine (Noradrenaline), or serotonin (5-hydroxytrytomine), all of which are believed to be heavily involved in regulating emotional stability, energy, appetite, and sleep. When these chemicals are no longer regulated in the way that our bodies intend, it's not hard to see how things can go haywire. This is the chemical story, and as a contained loop it is nearly complete. Identify the chemical, consume the treatment meant to address the imbalance (antidepressants), and wait for order to be restored. However it's far more complex than this, as everyone has their own unique experience and the psychiatrist has to take everything into account, including brain-scan patterns, to find the best treatment for their patients on an individual level.

In addition, one central question arises when thinking about things in this way: what causes these areas and pathways of the brain to malfunction? Is it idiopathic or do our lives have a role to play or both of the above? I believe our experiences, or rather, the way we respond to our experiences, can play a role in enhancing, alleviating, or even reversing certain emotional conditions. This was the truth in the outdated way of thinking about depression. It *was* true that depression often showed itself as an inappropriate emotional response to something that had happened or was happening in a person's life. Just because we now thankfully understand the chemical nature of that response does not mean that the human, experiential aspect of depression should be dismissed from our thinking. Regardless of chemicals, it is fairly logical for a person who is going through depression or anxiety to ask: what methods can be employed to better interact with the stresses of one's life?

The neurochemical and nontraditional mindful approaches to treating disorders like depression do not have to be two separate sides of the coin. The scientific knowledge of the underlying mechanisms of neurodegenerative movement disorders like Parkinson's Disease or psychosomatic disorders is starting to significantly overlap with the mechanisms that scientists associate with spirituality, particularly with regard to various forms of meditation or transcendence.

That concept of transcendence could very well be that meeting ground. It's the trait in people that accounts for their capacity or inclination to be "spiritual," which may be based on various chemical levels in our brain. These chemicals may dictate whether or not a person can become self-transcendent, meaning one can think or conceptualize beyond the barriers of one's own selfhood. More and more, I am coming to believe that individuals may have the power to actively affect these chemical levels ourselves by tapping into our inner selves and the power of meditation.

Let's go back to instinct, similar to the one that had earlier doctors linking depression with emotions based on experiences. I instinctively know that my spiritual mindfulness practices like meditation play a role in managing my emotional health. As a neurophysiologist by trade, I also know that my emotional health is largely based on neurotransmitters and the state of pathways in my brain. These two truths taken together lead me to believe that it's all connected. I believe the same pathways and neurochemicals involved in increasing our level of transcendence are the same pathways and neurochemicals that can make us anxious, or depressed, or stressed. If we also understand that these things can be triggered by our surrounding world (as they were with me), strengthening our inner selves through spiritual practice becomes a compelling solution to addressing our own brain chemistry.

Think of it purely in terms of that chemistry, as many of my scientific peers choose to do. If there is a significant imbalance of dopamine and serotonin levels, we become susceptible to a range of neurological disorders. Our goal, then, is to make sure that these neurotransmitters remain at levels that allow us to live healthy, functional lives. The challenge is that it's hard to know what these actual levels are since we can't directly measure the concentration of these neurotransmitters in the living brain. However the advancements in neuroimaging techniques enables the direct measurement of components of the neurotransmitter system, which can give us some idea of these neurotransmitters activity levels. Furthermore, the question is, can we control the levels of these crucial neurotransmitters, or is it purely down to the nature of our individual physiological systems? Can we practice behaviors that keep these neurotransmitters where they need to be? If we think its reasonable that the scientific evidence which suggests the same neurotransmitters or chemical levels are also closely associated with the trait known as transcendence, it's feasible to assume tending to our own transcendence through mindfulness practices like meditation may possibly be a way of maintaining our brain chemistry. Our spiritual health becomes very much conflated with our emotional health.

Several studies on the relationship between spirituality and emotional health suggest patients who are spiritual end up having better health outcomes, including less anxiety and depression. This makes sense to me especially since spiritual practices like meditation helps me to relax and become less anxious. Neuroimaging studies with subjects experienced in the practice of meditation show the activation of the prefrontal cortex and thalamus, as well as the inhibitory thalamic reticular nucleus and a resultant functional parietal lobe. This essentially may means that the anatomical change in our brains that occurs as a result of meditative practices may involves major neurotransmitter systems of our brain. These changes are key contributors in reducing anxiety and other symptoms of depression. Meditation, we're learning, is more than just spiritual; it's considered by some to be psychotogenic.

This is about more than just ameliorating symptoms once they appear; it's also about maintaining levels of these essential chemicals so that harmful brain disorders don't have a chance to develop in the first place. To this end, a group of scientists examined the dopaminergic tone of people who suffer from Parkinson's, who also practice Yoga Nidra. A study by Kjaer TW *et al* in 2002 suggests an increase in endogenous release of dopamine up to 65 percent with the patients practicing Yoga Nidra, returning this neurotransmitter to typical levels in these patient's brains. I immediately associate these findings with my knowledge of a depletion of dopamine from the striatum of over 65 percent before the cardinal symptoms of PD appear. Furthermore, while I would like to make such an obvious link between these findings and PD, I know based on my experience it's not that simple and I'm definitely not implying Yoga is a cure for PD. Conversely, this study encourages me because scientists now have technology to explore how these nontraditional practices can alter not just the physiology of the brain but the neurochemicals as well. Even though much more research is required, to me the studies suggest an important point: taking up and honing spiritual practices could possibly be more than just a coping mechanism for the negativity in our lives; it could also be a key way to keep our brains preemptively healthy.

I'd like to take this thought a step further, to a space where there is admittedly only a hint of scientific evidence to support my claim. I am convinced that all this same neurophysiology we've been discussing can also be linked to our spiritual practices. It has been a great joy to discover that, in my lifelong quest for spiritual alignment, nontraditional practices like meditation have helped to manage my negative emotions, raise my energy vibrations, and bring me to a state of mind where I can function and stay connected to the external world. This functioning as a result of these practices could extend beyond just our emotions or mental states.

These mindfulness practices are being integrated into treatment pathways for people with certain movement disorders or psychosomatic disorders, as well as oncology treatments. For example, the Mayo Clinic offers medicine programs that include meditation and acupuncture, integrated into more traditional treatment pathways and which are seen as complementary to more standard practices. The Mayo Clinic believes in treating patients holistically, and to them the human spirit is very much a part of that approach.

A lot of this, as always, has to do with pain. When experiencing pain, the mind can trigger the temporary override of physiological pain pathways in certain situations; according to the gate-control theory of pain put forth by Melzack and Wall, the brain is able to subconsciously wall off pain in certain areas from being able to reach the central nervous system; in other words, our brains do have a say in which parts of us hurt. It's a common line of thought that the brain is far more powerful than we think, and possesses capabilities to which we do not have conscious access. These nontraditional practices like meditation, acupuncture, and yoga are all geared toward becoming more in touch with our subconscious.

Yes, spirituality and many of the practices it entails are geared around "feeling good," as it is often dismissively put.

But the definition of "feeling good" is expanding to include real health benefits; as such it very well might be time to start thinking of our spiritual selves in the same we think about our diets, our exercise regimens, or any of the other habits we use to maintain or body's well-being.

Spirituality is innately personal. We all have unique souls at different stages of our individual journeys, which means discussing how various spiritual or mindful practices affect us personally can be less than adequate for others, because there's no guarantee that something I find useful for myself will be useful for you. However, personal experience still works as the best means of communicating with others about how we've managed to find our way, and can serve to shine a light on places where other people could perhaps look to find answers of their own. Hence I'd like to return to my own story.

As mentioned earlier, I now feel certain that I spent a very large portion of my young life ignoring toxic stress as well as depression. Part of ignoring this comes down to how I am wired, or how I felt at the time I had to be wired: when faced with an obstacle, the only option I saw was to discount its severity, push it away, and push forward as hard as I could. Even in the face of mounting symptoms like anxiety, headaches, fatigue, irritable bowels, and weight loss, my plan remained the same. I was attempting to be Superwoman, all things to all people, and we saw how that ended up. To this day I still experience irritable bowels, and once a year, without fail, I lose my voice. Permanent damage, however manageable, had been done. We cannot run from our brains forever.

In a way, I literally was trying to run from these things. It's fairly common for people like me to turn to strenuous exercise as a means of stabilizing our moods. Exercise has been proven to do this. Hard physical activity decreases cortisol levels and triggers the natural release of endorphins, a feel-good hormone commonly linked to feelings of euphoria. That euphoric sensation is important; it's very similar to the feeling associated with the effects of taking an antidepressant to increase serotonin and dopamine. It's also an end result of a good meditation session, which as we've talked about can raise our levels of those same chemicals.

Endorphins also serve to reduce anxiety, which was great for someone like me during that phase in my life. I was pushing as hard as could all the time, and being able to tap into exercise as a coping mechanism fit the mindset I was applying toward all my other endeavors.

Exercise was great, and it's still a major part of my routine for keeping my mind, spirit, and body stable. But it wasn't enough. This was a time when my body was breaking down as a result of ignored stress; as my body wore out, it would have made much more sense to also incorporate techniques that slowed myself, calmed myself, made me still. Sometimes the answer is not to exert yourself further, a lesson that people like me often have trouble learning. The answer sometimes is simply to be still and tap into your source energy—the universe. I did learn it, and now meditation is a key part of spiritual routine.

Keeping still is hard for someone whose instincts say to be constantly in motion. I have taught myself to sit quietly, if only for a few minutes, taking deep, controlled breaths while praying and meditating on the very idea of stillness. As I sit in an active attempt to shut out the external world for this brief period, meditation always bring me back to a place of peace. Sometimes this happens right away, during sessions when I'm grateful just to have carved out the time to sit still in the first place. Other times it's more of a process, focusing further and further on my own spirit until I can feel the peace within it.

The sensation is one of being lifted, eventually raised high enough that I feel bolstered and capable of getting out and facing the world. My mind might start cloudy during these sessions, and feelings of negativity may try to seep in. I have developed what I consider to be "counterchatter," or an opposing voice that takes those negative feelings, examines them, and asks, "is this really your reality?"

Often a physical sign appears, in the form of either a person or a circumstance. This sign directly takes on my questions, those feelings of doubt about myself or my ability to take on my life. Each question, each fear, is answered in turn.

This can stop me in my tracks, leaving me smiling that the universe has responded to my cry. The universe, my

God, has never and will never forsake me no matter how many times I want to give in or give up. It's a feeling of surrender, in the end. Surrendering to what is, to accepting one's circumstances while also understanding that it's temporary and they can be overcome. The quest for spiritual enlightenment, especially through meditation, is not truly about blocking out one's busy life. It's about stepping away from that life for just a brief period, examining it from a small distance, and realizing that each part of it is a necessary step in my soul's journey. This in itself brings me a sense of peace, not from knowing that I've escaped my life, but that I don't need to, that God intends for me to be right here, where I am.

These experiences brought on by meditation do more than just provide momentary peace of mind, or release neurochemicals that tide us over for a while. This sort of activity actually has the capability to *change* our brains, not because there's something remarkable about meditation, but because our brains are always changing.

This is due to a quality known as "plasticity." Essentially, this means that our brains are influenced by our experiences. As I mentioned in previous chapters, my PhD research explored how acute and/or chronic changes to sensory inputs into the brain can cause the functional properties of the associated neuronal networks to alter accordingly. If a certain pathway in the brain experiences a high volume of stimuli over time, those networks will begin to strengthen to accommodate that increased traffic. By the same token, if certain sensory inputs experience less stimuli, they'll weaken.

That sounds fairly opaque until we apply it to concepts like depression. FMRI studies and PET scans have visibly shown a decrease in volume in certain structures like the hippocampus, the prefrontal cortex, or the amygdala in brains that have been diagnosed with recurring depression. Other anxiety-related disorders, like Post Traumatic Stress Disorder (PTSD), are associated with changes in the hippocampus too, along with increased levels of the stress hormone cortisol, which can play a role in all kinds of other psychiatric disorders as well.

So, these disorders change the structure of our brains. They make certain neuronal networks larger or more active, and can make the size of different structures fluctuate. This plasticity comes as a response to what's happening in our brains, which as we've seen comes as a chemical response to how we are experiencing the world around us, and how we are reacting to our own lives.

Meditation is an experience that we control; that control actually lies at the heart of the practice, since much of its success hinges on our ability to actively separate ourselves from outside stimuli. And since meditation also accesses the same parts of the brain that are considered to be plastic, it too can shape our brains, just like all the stimuli coming from sources outside ourselves.

Meditation has been shown to modify the functional properties of the brain associated with negative moods, as well as our sense of well-being. With this in mind, I feel all the more confident in its ability to positively impact my life and the lives of others. By tapping into my unconscious through mindfulness practices, there is a strong possibility that I'm modulating my brain through innocuous stimuli, modifying it to rectify the symptoms of toxic stress. Our experiences shape our brains; meditation offers us a chance to turn that change in a direction that can help us live more emotionally stable lives.

If being mindful can take advantage of the plastic nature of our brains, it's also important to understand all the practices that could be considered mindful or spiritual. There's one human activity so commonplace that most people almost never think of it as something meditative or spiritual, and yet it has profound effects on our emotional states and our brain chemistry.

Few things interact with the brain's plastic nature quite like the foods we consume. Tons of common knowledge exist about how food and eating can affect our bodies, and yet very little of that discussion ends up focused on the brain. Similar to how meditation is the practice of actively deciding what stimuli are allowed into our minds for a given period of time, eating presents that same choice: we have control over what goes into our bodies, and yet so often we choose incorrectly.

Most of us are clearheaded about what inflammatory foods like sugar and wheat can have on our stomachs. I experienced this firsthand during the toxically stressful period of my life. We know how bloating feels, or how uncomfortable irritable bowels are. Our stomachs and digestive systems do not exist in a vacuum; they're deeply connected to our nervous systems. And neurologists are now coming across evidence that suggests the same foods that make us feel bad digestively can also have inflammatory effects on the brain.

Some neurologists have shown that eliminating inflammatory foods in the early stages of Alzheimer's can actually slow down the degeneration of neurons. While more substantial evidence is required to support this theory, it's still good news, and points to that strong connection between food and brain, but it's also reactionary; in that scenario, a person's diet isn't changed until symptoms present themselves. With movement disorders like Parkinson's, in which symptoms don't present themselves until a chemical imbalance has already hit a critical point, waiting and reacting isn't an option. Instead, treating our eating habits as part of our spiritual regimen could mean that we're bolstering the structures of our brains to prevent disorders and imbalances in the first place.

"Trust your gut." We've all heard the phrase, and it became a real mantra of mine when I realized that I needed to make changes to my approach to life. The gut, actually, is worth trusting: it practically has a mind of its own, an "enteric nervous system" that includes the complex array of neurons in the esophagus, stomach, small intestine, and colon. These are the neurons allow us not to have to actively focus on functions like digestion.

These gut neurons communicate using the same chemical signals as our brains. Our stomachs respond to stress just like our brains do—it can selectively shut down functions, and is the cause of many stress-related symptoms like mild gas or stomachaches. If we view meditation as something that better prepares our brains to handle the stress of our lives, than eating correctly should be considered just as mindful, because our stomachs are a key part of our stress response too. Avoiding inflammatory foods can have a directly positive effect on our moods and our ability to cope with stress.

When we eat inflammatory foods, the constant inflammation weakens the tight junctions between the cells lining the gastrointestinal tract, which are crucial for protecting the body from toxins. When those junctions break down, that barrier becomes compromised, and partially digested food particles enter our circulatory systems. These particles are viewed as attackers by the immune system, which then releases a cascade of proteins called cytokines to fend them off. These cytokines, while useful in protecting our bodies from invaders, are also highly inflammatory, and are directly tied to ailments like depression and anxiety. Those who are impacted by these problems have been proven to have much higher circulating levels of cytokines than people with balanced brain chemistry.

For myself, I knew that I would never achieve spiritual and mental wellness without changing my diet. I cut out what we traditionally call "junk food," but even that wasn't quite enough, as I was still experiencing many of the same stress-related stomach symptoms. I eliminated wheat from my diet, which helped within a week and wasn't that difficult, given the wide variety of wheat alternatives available. Giving up meat was a little trickier, since I was left with a lot of foods that weren't that healthy and didn't sustain me. I was putting on weight due to the high carb and sugar intake, and so I sought more change. I am now a 100-percent gluten-free pescatarian, as fish is a great source of protein and is easy to find at restaurants. I drink decaffeinated herbal tea and water, with alcohol rarely thrown in (it triggers hot flushes!). I'm also eliminating diary produce as well. I crafted my diet based on how I was feeling, and the process over time felt very similar to the ways in which I was working to improve my spiritual life as well.

I began treating my stomach like I treated my brain, using meditation and careful eating in tandem to better tend to my inner self. These things, along with exercise, have all become part of an equation that places me in a more spiritual frame of mind on a daily basis, a frame of mind that allows me to be more receptive to my spirit guides. When I work actively to give my mind and body peace that newly created space allows me to listen, in ever sense of the word. Now that I'm more spiritually receptive, I can get back to thinking about and seeking answers to the questions of my life. My journey, my soul, my purpose.

There's a way to look at this where it all seems severe. Much of my story and this book has been about struggle, about how we can use certain practices to stave off pain and suffering through spirituality and mindfulness. For me, there certainly have been some battles for wellness, however I don't think that's the whole story, or even most of it. The real reason I've turned to spirituality and the neuroscience that underpins it is my search for meaning and purpose. Why am I the way that I am? What is the purpose of this journey I'm on?

Given how much time I've spent mired in toxic stress, anxiety, and depression, I've also spent significant time in prayer and meditation wondering why these things were placed in my path. The journey of my soul is meant to teach me something in this life, so that I can progress and evolve to the next spiritual level. I'm here to learn and teach others, just as my young brother Anthony was for the brief time that he was here with us.

I have found meaning in my depression. When I think of my life and the challenges I've pursued, so much of it was instigated by my pursuit of spiritual and mental wellness. I've been around the world seeking spiritual answers, and have spent who knows how many hours in a lab learning about the science of the brain, even when surrounded by others who would discount me because of the color of my skin. This motivation had to have come from somewhere. I believe it came from my thirst for spirituality combined with the mental restlessness that comes from the negativity of depression.

When I feel myself slipping into a negative mood, I now know to look inward and focus on connecting with the universe through prayer and meditation. My suffering, when coupled with my mindful and spiritual habits, leads me to seek ways to transfer my negative energy into something positive. My work becomes a focal point, pouring myself into the value I believe exists in the medical-technology field I've chosen.

Part of my healing is pouring my heart and soul into my community. I try to give back as much as I can to others whenever I can, to help to make a difference in people's lives. It is highly rewarding to help someone move from a life of struggle or being disadvantaged to one of overcoming those odds. It feeds my soul and gives me purpose. I strongly believe in equity for all, and it's my responsibility to work hard toward that end. I take that responsibility seriously no matter what my circumstance or emotional state of well-being.

Even this book is an outpouring of that energy, a new benchmark in my acceptance that my depression is mine. Depression forces me to continually seek refuge in my spirituality, with my energy, my guides, and the universe. It took several years of work to build the courage or peace within myself to be open about depression. Masking it for all this time has been near impossible, and as I've learned, was causing me harm.

True to form, the universe has worked out for me. My hard work was met with opportunities and resources that would allow me to focus on my self-development during a time I needed it most, both spiritually and professionally. I think of the Bush Fellowship I received in 2014, a grant designed to increase leadership in Minnesota by making investments in people who have demonstrated exceptional community-leadership ability. The fellowship comes with enormous flexibility, and allows its Fellows to articulate what they need to become a better leader, whether through a self-designed learning experience or an academic program. Quite simply, they provide the resources and support to help a person "make it happen."

What a gift for someone like me, who had spent so much of her life self-designing experiences meant to improve herself. The Fellowship encouraged me to take time out of my busy lifestyle to focus on my own wellbeing. It provided me with the resources to hire an executive coach, Wrisë, a wonderful lady based in California who worked with me holistically on all my development needs. Wrisë was enormously helpful, and she deepened my understanding of the importance of aligning all facets of my life with my spiritual path, even when it's uncomfortable, even when it takes courage. In short, I had been given exactly what I needed. I'd been fueled by a spiritual restlessness my whole life, and it was now coming together.

All this time fighting to dismantle stereotypes, climb over obstacles, pursue my career and self-development even as I was subjugating my own spirit—it has come to fruition, for me. There will always be battles, many of which I can envision and some I surely cannot. I am constantly readying myself. I'm learning, and trying to make the most of this journey I'm on.

That's all insular, within myself. My soul is not here just to better itself, but to help others learn and grow as well. This desire to help has also proven to be a key outlet for my negative emotions, a space where I can turn dark feeling into something light. I do everything I can to support my community here in the Twin Cities. The stark social, racial, and economic disparities that exist in Minnesota are surprising and depressing, and I've made it my mission to help those who have been given far less than they deserve. Being with my people, helping to build vibrant, healthy communities, and seeing the quality of their lives improve from a state of dependency to independence is one of the great joys of my life. It shifts my energy from a place of low energy to one of high.

I think of how I felt in those labs and those early work experiences, when some of my peers would have loved to see me fail as a damning indictment of all women of color. That pressure of striving to be the exception to the rule while also changing the rule. Part of that work was done back then, when I *did* succeed, when I *did* persevere and obtain the career that I wanted. However, part of that work is still in front of me, as I now turn my attention toward those who might try to follow in my path. New examples of this success happen all the time; I was one of them, and there have been many since. Now I see that part of my spiritual journey is to make sure that the people trying to follow those examples have the resources and circumstances they need to do so. Someone had been there for me when I needed to "make it happen." It's my turn to do that for someone else, some other soul on a journey like mine.

Many of those journeys are like mine, because emotional health is a major issue in the underprivileged communities I work with. A disproportionate amount of the population suffers from depression and anxiety. Worse, large swaths of these communities do not have access to healthcare, and many who do choose not to enroll because a complete breakdown in trust toward our healthcare system. Others are too afraid to address their problems; as we've talked about, emotional health and depression are highly stigmatized. Another challenge is access to organic foods. Natural, earth-grown foods can be far too expensive for the people in most desperate need of making nutritional changes. These are large challenges that will require widespread effort to enact solutions, but there are ways to begin.

As science proves that practices in mindfulness can help alleviate or manage symptoms of depression, these techniques that I've come to value so highly could be put to great use in these places. A person does not have to engage with the healthcare system to meditate. They don't have to cultivate a fully functioning urban garden just to cut preservatives or unnatural sugars. The mind is an incredibly powerful organ, one that we will probably never fully understand. And yet, we do have control over it, through simple changes in behavior. Those changes could make the difference in a person's life, even when they can't necessarily get to a doctor or shop organically. I know the power of mindfulness and all that it entails. It's personal. I've lived it.

Every day I wake up asking God to show me my path and purpose. By requesting this out loud, by taking that throwaway moment and making it real and tangible, my intentions are planted in the universe. This helps me stay connected to my quest. When I doubt myself and I'm feeling negative, I am now better prepared to at least try to return myself to a space of positivity.

That "positivity," as we've seen, is more profound than just good feeling. I'm referring to the headspace carved out using all these mindful behaviors that allows me to function as I know I'm supposed to. When I'm eating correctly and exercising and meditating, the result is that I see more clearly—see myself, my own spirit, and the opportunities all around me.

The more that neuroscientists learn about the brain, the smaller that "stretch" between spiritual practices and bodily health becomes. As that connection becomes more and more apparent, it only makes sense that a heightened understanding of neuroscience could be put toward concepts like meditation and prayer. I would not have survived, let alone thrived in the ways that I have, without this deep connection. That's not to say that science and spirituality overlap completely: spirituality will never tell me about the way my body and brain biologically function. That's a question of science. The questions that follow that scientific understanding, that synthesis—those are perhaps best handled by examining our spiritual selves. We are more than just our bodies and our mixture of neurochemicals. As we step beyond this reductive view and into questions of meaning, purpose, and journeys, we need tools beyond science to complement that underpinning knowledge.

There's nothing radical in that thought. We're talking about techniques that do a little bit each day to give peace to our spirits and bolster our bodies against imbalance. They're small things that, over time, can have major impacts. These are the techniques that become habit, which then become a cultivated spiritual presence that can pull us through the darkest periods of our lives, as it did for me. My depression is and will always be a gift. It's the force in my life that pushes me to finally take care of myself, to seek answers in both spirituality and scientific academia, and to use those answers to affect others on their own paths.

EPILOGUE

I often think about the confusion I felt when my little brother was taken away from me at such a young age and what this experience was like for my mother. When my firstborn, my son, was born, I was elated and enjoyed each moment watching him grow. As my love for him grew deeper and deeper with each day that passed, my mind would wonder to my little brother. I was fearful when my son approached this age, and prayed he would not be taken from me as well. As I witnessed my son walk, start to talk, and be inquisitive about his surroundings, developing a little personality of his own, I was at times beside myself with anxiety thinking how my mother experienced the same for Anthony only to have him suddenly snatched away at the tender age of fifteen months. These thoughts never left me. The closer Andrew got to that age I would watch him closely, even checking on him obsessively throughout the night to make sure he was breathing. I was so relieved when Andrew passed this age and continued to grow well into his toddler years. I realize now my brother Anthony's short lifetime sparked a spiritual curiosity within me. I unconsciously embarked upon my spiritual journey, which would take me deep inside myself.

I'm very reflective even when it's hard for me, especially revisiting some of the most painful moments of my life. I very easily could have never slowed down, never reflected, and kept pushing to that point of burnout and beyond. It wouldn't have been hard to slip into that; all it would have taken was a little less urgent interest in my own purpose or a little more skepticism in my ability to tap into something spiritual inside of me. I very well could have been the sort of neuroscientist unconcerned with anything beyond the physics and chemistry of the brain. There's enough there to fill a lifetime of study, and with my drive, I could thrown myself purely into that pursuit.

I wasn't entirely like that, and I still am not. I was not just a woman striving to make it in a field that wasn't entirely comfortable having her around, though that's certainly a life that requires endless amounts of focus and energy. I also experienced emotional challenges and as I evolved spiritually I came to view my depression as a gift—a driving motivation for spiritual enlightenment and service.

That service part is critical. My spiritual reflection has shown me the value of bringing my full self to my work with others, not just my professional self. The goal, whether I'm at my job at Medtronic or in my community helping others on their journey, is to become a "transformational progressive leader." A transformational leader uses a heightened sense of spiritual awareness in order to align their being with their purpose, using that unification to guide others in a compassionate, heartfelt way. I know as well as anyone the impact this sort of leader can have on others: MAJ was a transformational leader who saw something in me before I saw it myself.

Now, it's time for me to be the one who helps to transforms others. By the time I arrived in Minnesota in 2010, I knew that service would be an essential part of my soul's journey in the USA. I immediately got involved with the African American Leadership Forum (AALF), an organization designed to address the disparities felt by black people in our community. Minnesota has the largest academic-achievement gap between white and brown children in the country, as well as incredibly high economic and health disparities. This is a state that I love despite these problems; it is my home. I am intent on contributing to closing those gaps in every way that I can.

The area in which I'm best able to contribute my expertise is in strategy creation, process application, and structure. Here I'm able to take the skills I use all the time at Medtronic and offer them to my community as well. After a few months of this work, a senior executive from a MN-based Fortune-500 company called me at work. At first I was nervous, but she soon asked if I'd be willing to replace her as co-chair of AALF education workgroup. The opportunity, surely a spiritual blessing, was tremendous. It was rewarding work that let me problem-solve with elected officials and organizational heads, and put me in contact with reformists of all kinds who were as intent as I was in improving our community.

I've written a lot about the various spiritual ideas and techniques I've explored throughout my life. My spirit guides have been beyond lifesaving for me, as have the many people the universe placed in my path throughout my journey. I've been explored how to meditate more effectively, and put a considerable amount of trial and error into eating mindfully to take better care of myself. I've read countless spiritual, mindful books, and will keep seeking to learn about more practices I can adopt to become more enlightened. I am certain that my own path to learning about the nature of my soul will never end. I will be reading and meditating until the day my soul transitions from this lifetime, and I'll be working to help others do the same.

The heartbeat of this book has been to point out the two sides between spirituality and neuroscience is much less combative than some might think. I'd like to explicitly take that connection a step further. One of the most spiritual acts available to me in this life has been my scientific study.

How could it not be? If a key part of spirituality is the quest to understand ourselves and how we fit into the universe, isn't the first step understanding ourselves, what we're made of, how we work? I did develop a comfort with the many spiritual practices in my life in spite of being a neuroscientist; furthermore, I discovered them primarily *because* of my study of the brain, and used that same scientific curiosity to pursue spiritual ideas that could be laid on top of that science. I am better at meditation because of my understanding of how it affects us neurologically; I am a mindful eater because I am familiar with the complex neuronal network in our digestive systems. Looking back, the time I spent in labs doing research was not only something that was happening at the same time as my spiritual journey. It was *part* of my spiritual journey. The inner peace I associate with my mindfulness habits would simply not be as robust without my knowledge of the science that underpins it.

Think of that initial dynamic laid out regarding study of the brain: the more we learn about it, the more we realize we have yet to understand. One question gets answered, and two spring up in its place. It's a process less about finding true answers and more about learning what the correct questions are, so that we can continue searching.

Doesn't this sound an awful lot like a spiritual journey? When it's put this way, doesn't it seem slightly absurd these two realms of thought have stood in opposition for so long? In my life, that line has become blurred to the point of being barely noticeable. I meditate, I pray, I read, I studied the brain. These behaviors no longer sit on two separate lists.

The combination, as I see it, provides a truly comprehensive way of examining ourselves and others, as well as learning how to better help each other. Right now, there is a person somewhere who has been relegated to a hospital bed because the toxic stress of their life became too much in that moment to bear. Certain neuronal pathways have been blocked, neurotransmitters are out of balance, and perhaps even their stomach is responding to the stress by partially shutting down function. These are medical problems, biology problems.

But this person is perhaps also struggling in ways that aren't as easy to put into chemical terms. Maybe, like me, she has suffered a tremendous loss of some kind in her family, and is now trying to outwork that gnawing feeling in her spirit to the point of exhaustion. Maybe she's lonely, or depressed, or anxious, or worried she's not living up to her own vision of herself. These are things that put people in hospitals too. It seems quite obvious that this woman requires treatment that rolls an understanding of her own neurochemistry into a way for her to address the more purpose-based questions she has about her life. That, if she is going to avoid ending up in this bed again, she might need to focus on the needs of her spirit as much as her body.

That's a hypothetical. My life, however, isn't, nor are the lives of the people in my community that I've been drawn to help by understanding what my role is in my own journey. The universe gave me a tremendous amount of gifts, and whether or not I'm using them to the fullest is a difficult question to answer. Where would I be, had it not been for the many people and guides who came into my life to help me learn how to use them? Would I be using them at all?

Part of using these gifts must be helping others discover theirs. Or maybe just help them find a little peace of mind to make it through a tough day without breaking down. Or furthermore just help them feel a little more hope in the face of emotional-health problems that afflict far more of them than they'll ever admit.

A central part of this mission, as it certainly was for me, is education. So often a tool manipulated by oppressors, education lies at the heart of improving the lives of the people in the communities that need it most. I was given the opportunity to do so when asked me to chair a new public charter school called Mastery in partnership with Minneapolis Public Schools. I was of course eager to help out in the opening and governance of the school in every way that I could.

These are highly mobile students in high-poverty areas, too many homeless, far too much on free or reduced lunch. Despite the narrative, lo and behold, when given the attention they deserved and immersed in an environment of belief, they thrive in this rich academic environment. Building on a twenty-six-year legacy of a successful school network called the Harvest Network of schools, the new school now is in its fourth year, serving students from kindergarten through fourth grade. However, the vision is greater than these three schools. The long-term plan is to create a school district in North Minneapolis that serves 3,800 students by the year 2025. It's as worthy a goal as any in my life, and I'll work with school leaders and the district however I can to make this possible.

I've been lucky enough to think even more broadly, reach even further. Through AALF I attended many forums. Seminars and congresses including the Congressional Black Caucus, where along with a small Twin Cities AALF delegation we met with our congressman and senators who outlined their legislative agendas. We heard about how their proposed policies might affect those most in need back in Minnesota.

It was a necessary and profound moment for all of us in attendance; the conference was held amidst growing national attention to unjust killings in America, as well as the recent Supreme Court decision to invalidate a major portion of the Voting Rights Act. The moment could easily have felt hopeless, but instead we renewed our focus and commitment to correcting the social injustices we were seeing unfold. I was keen to hear talk of issues and movements like the Fight for 15, criminal injustices, and affordable healthcare. Some stories were heart wrenching and painful, while at the same time inspiring. I was privileged to attend the awards dinner in the company of 44th President of the United States- Barak Obama and his wife former First Lady Michelle Obama— they are inspiring. I left the conference with energy, hope, and the feeling that I was capable and willing to do what was necessary to tackle the problems facing so many people in my community.

All of it led to the same questions as ever, this time asked with more fervor: why am I here? Why I am blessed to be in the presence of so many people who share commitment and passion, and what am I supposed to do with my experience and the experience of those around me?

I haven't answered these questions in full yet. I know, however, that I am becoming a better leader. At the center of this is being in touch with my spiritual side, tending to it, making sure that as my mind opens itself to new experiences that my spiritual self is growing as well. I've been a spiritual person for as long as I can remember. Now I am seeing where this path leads: home, to my community, where I can aid them in becoming who they're meant to be and have them, in turn, transform me.

I think back to that moment in Puerto Rico, when I felt God so clearly as I jotted in that notepad trying to capture it, feeling impossibly aware of the sights and sounds around me like I'd never been before. It was a moment of pure elation and calmness, not because of any extraordinary truth being revealed to me, for a moment, I was able to be fully present. In that brief instant, my suffering had led to a point of pure, ordinary joy.

That feeling of peace is obtainable. You can look at it as a glimpse of spiritual enlightenment, or you can look at it as a moment when you've worked hard and long enough on your own neurochemistry that for a second, things feel perfectly in balance. In their ways, both are true, and I've geared my life around the idea that pursuing both routes tends to make them blend together.

I will always be that little girl who turned inside herself when her brother passed away. I have not shed that identity, nor would I want to. In that moment, my brother's spiritual journey was intersecting with mine, setting me on a path that, while difficult, would prove to be the one· most conducive for my growth and my soul's evolution. Fueled by the sense that the uneasiness I was living with could no longer be ignored, I pursued that growth through scientific research, and I pursued that growth through careful attention to my spiritual side. In my mind, they are framed as two elements of the same path, the one along which I seek to understand myself.

References

Andrea Kübler, Boris Kotchoubey. (2007) "Brain–computer interfaces in the continuum of consciousness." *Current Opinion in Neurology* 20, 643-649. Online publication. 1-Dec-2007.

Bargh, J. A., & Chartrand, T. L. (1999). "The unbearable automaticity of being";_*American Psychologist*, 54 (7), 462.

Baron Short E, Kose S, Mu Q, Borckardt J, Newberg A, George MS, Kozel FA. (2010) "Regional brain activation during meditation shows time and practice effects: an exploratory FMRI study"; Evid Based Complement Alternat Med. 2010 Mar; 7(1):121-7. doi: 10.1093/ecam/nem163. Epub 2007 Dec 27.

Berger TW1, Hampson RE, Song D, Goonawardena A, Marmarelis VZ, Deadwyler SA. (2011) "cortical neural prosthesis for restoring and enhancing memory"; J Neural Eng. 2011 Aug;8(4):046017. Epub 2011 Jun 15

Bingham V, Habermann B. "The influence of spirituality on family management of Parkinson's disease." J Neurosci Nurs. 2006 Dec; 38(6): 422-7. PMID: 17233512

Bollen J, Trick L, Llewellyn D, Dickens C.; "The effects of acute inflammation on cognitive functioning and emotional processing in humans: A systematic review of experimental studies."; J Psychosom Res. 2017 Mar;94:47-55. doi: 10.1016/j.jpsychores.2017.01.002. Review. PMID: 28183402

Bota RG, Hazen J, Tieu R, Novac A. (2016) "Mindfulness-Based Cognitive Therapy for Patients With Depression Decreases the Need for Outpatient Visits." Prim Care Companion CNS Disord. 2016 Aug 25;18(4). doi: 10.4088/PCC.16m01985. PMID: 27828695

Brain Behav Immun. 2017 Jan 25. pii: S0889-1591(17)30016-8. doi: 10.1016/j.bbi.2017.01.016. [Epub ahead of print] Review. PMID: 28131791

Breuer, J., & Freud, S. (1895). "Studies on hysteria." Standard Edition 2: London.

Cosimo Urgesi, Salvatore M. Aglioti, Miran Skrap, and Franco Fabbro (2010); "The Spiritual Brain: Selective Cortical Lesions Modulate Human Self Transcendence"; Neuron 65, 309-319, February 11, 2010 de Jong M, Lazar SW, Hug K, Mehling WE, Hölzel BK, Sack AT, Peeters F, Ashih H, Mischoulon D, Gard T. (2016), "Effects of Mindfulness-Based Cognitive Therapy on Body Awareness in Patients with Chronic Pain and Comorbid Depression." Front Psychol. 2016 Jun 30;7:967. doi: 10.3389/fpsyg.2016.00967. PMID: 27445929

Desbordes G1, Negi LT, Pace TW, Wallace BA, Raison CL, Schwartz EL. (2012) "Effects of mindful-attention and compassion meditation training on amygdala response to emotional stimuli in an ordinary, non-meditative state." Front Hum Neurosci. 2012 Nov 1;6:292. doi: 10.3389/fnhum.2012.00292. eCollection 2012.

E. Mohandas, M.D.; Mens Sana Monogr. 2008 Jan-Dec; 6(1): 63–80: Neurobiology of Spirituality doi: 10.4103/0973-1229.33001; PMCID: PMC3190564

Farb N, Segal ZV, Mayberg H, Bean J, McKeon D, Fatima Z, Anderson AK. (2007) "Attending to the present: mindfulness meditation reveals distinct neural modes of self-reference." Soc Cogn Affect Neurosci. 2007 Dec;2(4):313-22. doi: 10.1093/scan/nsm030. PMID: 18985137

Farb N, Anderson AK, Mayberg H, Bean J, McKeon D, Segal ZV (2010) "Minding one's emotions: mindfulness training alters the neural expression of sadness."_Emotion. 2010 Feb;10(1):25-33. doi: 10.1037/a0017151.

Fayed N1, Lopez Del Hoyo Y, Andres E, Serrano-Blanco A, Bellón J, Aguilar K, Cebolla A, Garcia-Campayo J. (2013) "Brain changes in long-term zen meditators using proton magnetic resonance spectroscopy and diffusion tensor imaging: a controlled study"; PLoS One. 2013;8(3):e58476. doi: 10.1371/journal. pone.0058476. Epub 2013 Mar.

Filpa V, Moro E, rotasoni M, Crema F, Frigo G, Giaroni C; (2016) "Role of glutamatergic neurotransmission in the enteric nervous system and brain-gut axis in health and disease." Neuropharmacology. 2016 Dec; 111:14-33. doi: 10.1016/j.neuropharm.2016.08.024. Epub 2016 Aug 22

Folgueira C, Seoane LM, Casanueva FF; (2014) "The brain-stomach connection." Front Horm Res. 2014;42:83-92. doi: 10.1159/000358316. Review. PMID: 24732927

Fox K, Stryker M. "Integrating Hebbian and homeostatic plasticity: introduction." Philos Trans R Soc Lond B Biol Sci. 2017 Mar 5;372(1715). pii: 20160413.

Freud, S. (1915). "The unconscious." SE, 14: 159-204.

Freud, S. (1961). "The resistances to psychoanalysis." In The Standard Edition of the Complete Psychological

Works of Sigmund Freud, Volume XIX (1923-1925): The Ego and the Id and other works (pp. 211-224).

G Knight; (1972) "Neurosurgical aspects of psychosurgery." Proc R Soc Med. 1972 Dec; 65(12): 1099–1104. PMCID: PMC1644424

Garrison KA1, Scheinost D, Worhunsky PD, Elwafi HM, Thornhill TA 4th, Thompson E, Saron C, Desbordes G, Kober H, Hampson M, Gray JR, Constable RT, Papademetris X, Brewer JA;(2013) "Real-time fMRI links subjective experience with brain activity during focused attention"; Neuroimage. 2013 Nov 1;81:110-8. doi: 10.1016/j.neuroimage.2013.05.030. Epub 2013 May 17.

Greenwald, A. G., & Banaji, M. R. (1995). "Implicit social cognition: attitudes, self-esteem, and stereotypes." Psychological review, 102(1), 4.

Hajebrahimi B, Kiamanesh A, Asgharnejad Farid AA, Asadikaram G. (2016) "Type 2 diabetes and mental disorders; a plausible link with inflammation." Cell Mol Biol (Noisy-le-grand). 2016 Nov 30; 62(13):71-77. doi: 10.14715/cmb/2016.62.13.13. Review. PMID: 28040067

Harat M1, Rudas M, Rybakowski J, (2008) "Psychosurgery: the past and present of ablation procedures." Neuro Endocrinol Lett. 2008 Nov; 29 Suppl 1:105-22.

Hilton L, Hempel S, Ewing BA, Apaydin E, Xenakis L, Newberry S, Colaiaco B, Maher AR, Shanman RM, Sorbero ME, Maglione MA; "Mindfulness Meditation for Chronic Pain: Systematic Review and Meta-analysis." Ann Behav Med. 2016 Sep 22. [Epub ahead of print]. PMID: 27658913

Hölzel BK1, Carmody J, Vangel M, Congleton C, Yerramsetti SM, Gard T, Lazar SW. (2011). "Mindfulness practice leads to increases in regional brain gray matter density." Psychiatry Res. 2011 Jan 30;191(1):36-43. doi: 10.1016/j.pscychresns.2010.08.006. Epub 2010 Nov 10.

Jevning R, Anand R, Biedebach M, Fernando G. (1996) "Effects on regional cerebral blood flow of transcendental meditation." Physiol Behav. 1996 Mar;59(3):399-402. PMID: 8700938.

Jonathan R Wolpaw, Niels Birbaumer, Dennis J McFarland, Gert Pfurtscheller, Theresa M Vaughan (2002) "Brain–computer interfaces for communication and control"; Clinical Neurophysiology June 2002 Volume 113, Issue 6, Pages 767–791

Kabat-Zinn J, Massion AO, Kristeller J, Peterson LG, Fletcher KE, Pbert L, et al. (1992) "Effectiveness of a meditation-based stress reduction program in the treatment of anxiety disorders." American Journal of Psychiatry. 1992;19:936–43

Kasabov NK; NeuCube (2014): "a spiking neural network architecture for mapping, learning and understanding of spatio-temporal brain data"; 2014 Apr;52:62-76. doi: 10.1016/j.neunet.2014.01.006. Epub 2014 Jan 20

Khan F, Oloketuyi SF, (2017) "A future perspective on neurodegenerative diseases: nasopharyngeal and gut microbiota"; J Appl Microbiol. 2017 Feb;122(2):306-320. doi: 10.1111/jam.13327. Epub 2016 Nov 21.

Kiecolt-Glaser JK, Fagundes CP, Andridge R, Peng J, Malarkey WB, Habash D, Belury MA. (2016) "Depression, daily stressors and inflammatory responses to high-fat meals: when stress overrides healthier food choices." Mol Psychiatry. 2016 Sep 20. doi: 10.1038/mp.2016.149. PMID: 27646264

Kjaer TW, Bertelsen C, Piccini P, Brooks D, Alving J, Lou HC. (2002) "Increased dopamine tone during meditation-induced change of consciousness." Brain Res Cogn Brain. (2002);13(2):255–259.

Kohler O, Krogh J, Mors O, Benros ME, "Inflammation in Depression and the Potential for Anti-Inflammatory Treatment"; Curr Neuropharmacol. 2016;14(7):732-42. Review. PMID: 27640518

Lazar SW, Kerr CE, Wasserman RH, Gray JR, Greve DN, Treadway MT, McGarvey M, Quinn BT, Dusek JA, Benson H, Rauch SL, Moore CI, Fischl B. (2005) "Meditation experience is associated with increased cortical thickness." Neuroreport. 2005;16(17):1893–1897.[PMCID: PMC1361002] [PubMed: 16272874]

Leonard BE; (2017) "Inflammation and depression: a causal or coincidental link to the pathophysiology?" Acta Neuropsychiatr. 2017 Jan 23:1-16. doi: 10.1017/neu.2016.69. [Epub ahead of print]

Liang SF, Shaw FZ, Young CP, Chang DW, Liao YC; (2010) "A closed-loop brain computer interface for real-time seizure detection and control." Conf Proc IEEE Eng Med Biol Soc. 2010;2010:4950-3. doi: 10.1109/IEMBS.2010.5627243. PMID: 21096670

Luders E1, Toga AW, Lepore N, Gaser C. (2009) "The underlying anatomical correlates of long-term meditation: larger hippocampal and frontal volumes of gray matter." Neuroimage. 2009 Apr 15;45(3):672-8.

MacKenzie MB, Kocovski NL. (2016) "Mindfulness-based cognitive therapy for **depression**: trends and developments." Psychol Res Behav Manag. 2016 May 19;9:125-32. doi: 10.2147/PRBM.S63949.

Maczurek A1, Hager K, Kenklies M, Sharman M, Martins R, Engel J, Carlson DA, Münch G.; (2008) Adv Drug Deliv Rev. "Lipoic acid as an anti-inflammatory and neuroprotective treatment for Alzheimer's disease". 2008 Oct-Nov; 60(13-14):1463-70. doi: 10.1016/j.addr.2008.04.015. Epub 2008 Jul 4.

Madhukar H. Trivedi,(2004) "The Link Between Depression and Physical Symptoms"; Prim Care Companion J Clin Psychiatry 2004;6 [suppl 1]:12–16)

Mashour GA1, Walker EE, Martuza RL (2005) "Psychosurgery: past, present, and future," Brain Res Brain Res Rev. 2005 Jun;48(3):409-19.

Melzack R, Wall PD. Pain Mechanisms: "A New Theory." Science, 1965; 150(3699):971-979.

Monti DA, Kash KM, Kunkel EJ, Brainard G, Wintering N, Moss AS, Rao H, Zhu S, Newberg AB. (2012) "Changes in cerebral blood flow and anxiety associated with an 8-week mindfulness programme in women with breast cancer"; Stress Health. 2012 Dec;28(5):397-407. doi: 10.1002/smi.2470.

Nancy A. Craigmyle; "The beneficial effects of meditation: contribution of the anterior cingulate and locus coeruleus"; Front Psychol. 2013; 4: 731. Published online Oct 16, 2013.

Newberg AB, Wintering N, Waldman MR, Amen D, Khalsa DS, Alavi A. (2010) "Cerebral blood flow differences between long-term meditators and non-meditators." Conscious Cogn. 2010 Dec;19(4):899-905. doi: 10.1016/j.concog.2010.05.003. PMID: 20570534

Newberg AB1, Serruya M, Wintering N, Moss AS, Reibel D, Monti DA. (2014) "Meditation and neurodegenerative diseases"; Ann N Y Acad Sci. 2014 Jan;1307:112-23. doi: 10.1111/nyas.12187. Epub 2013 Aug 7.

Pagé MG, Watt-Watson J, Choinière M.(2017) "Do depression and anxiety profiles over time predict persistent post-surgical pain? A study in cardiac surgery patients"; Eur J Pain. 2017 Feb 10. doi: 10.1002/ejp.998. [Epub ahead of print] PMID: 28185371

Paul N, Stanton SJ, Greeson JM, Smoski MJ, Wang L. (2013) "Psychological and neural mechanisms of trait mindfulness in reducing depression vulnerability." Soc Cogn Affect Neurosci. 2013 Jan;8(1):56-64. doi: 10.1093/scan/nss070. Epub 2012 Jun 19.

Pickut B, Van Hecke W, Kerckhofs E, Mariën P, Vanneste S, Cras P, Parizel PM (2013): "Mindfulness based intervention in Parkinson's disease leads to structural brain changes on MRI: a randomized controlled longitudinal trial"; Clin Neurol Neurosurg. 2013 Dec;115(12):2419-25. doi: 10.1016/j. clineuro.2013.10.002. Epub 2013 Oct 16.

Ramgopal S, Thome-Souza S, Jackson M, Kadish NE, Sánchez Fernández I, Klehm J, Bosl W, Reinsberger C, Schachter S, Loddenkemper T._(2014) "Seizure detection, seizure prediction, and closed-loop warning systems in epilepsy"; Epilepsy Behav. 2014 Aug;37:291-307. doi: 10.1016/j.yebeh.2014.06.023. Review._PMID: 25174001

Rieder R, Wisniewski PJ, Alderman BL, Campbell SC. (2017) Microbes and mental health: A review." Brain Behav Immun. 2017 Jan 25. pii: S0889-1591(17)30016-8. doi: 10.1016/j.bbi.2017.01.016. [Epub ahead of print] Review.

Rolston JD, Gross RE, Potter SM. (2010) "Closed-loop, open-source electrophysiology." Front Neurosci. 2010 Sep 15;4. pii: 31. doi: 10.3389/fnins.2010.00031. PMID: 2085944

Rossini PM, Noris Ferilli MA, Ferreri F (2012) "Cortical plasticity and brain computer interface"; Eur J Phys Rehabil Med. 2012 Jun; 48(2):307-12.

Sakas DE, Panourias IG, Simpson BA. (2007) "An introduction to neural networks surgery; a field of neuromodulation which is based on advances in neural networks science and digitised brain imaging." Acta Neurochir Suppl. 2007; 97 (Pt 2):3-13. Review. PMID: 17691284

Saniotis A, Henneberg M, Kumaratilake J, Grantham JP.(2014) "Messing with the mind: evolutionary challenges to human brain augmentation." Front Syst Neurosci. 2014 Sep 30;8:152. doi: 10.3389/fnsys.2014.00152. eCollection 2014.

Segal ZV, Kennedy S, Gemar M, Hood K, Pedersen R, Buis T. (2006) "Cognitive reactivity to sad mood provocation and the prediction of depressive relapse." Archives of General Psychiatry. 2006;63:749–55.

Segal ZV, Williams JMG, Teasdale JD. (2002) "Mindfulness-based cognitive therapy for depression—A new approach to preventing relapse." New York, NY: Guilford Press. 2002

Smith R, Fass H, Lane RD; (2014) "Role of medial prefrontal cortex in representing one's own subjective emotional responses: a preliminary study." Conscious Cogn. 2014 Oct;29:117-30. doi: 10.1016/j.concog.2014.08.002

Smith R, Lane RD, (2016) "Unconscious emotion: A cognitive neuroscientific perspective"; Neurosci Biobehav Rev. 2016 Oct;69:216-38. doi: 10.1016/j.neubiorev.2016.08.013. Review. PMID: 27522011

Smith R, Lane RD. (2015) "The neural basis of one's own conscious and unconscious emotional states." Neurosci Biobehav Rev. 2015 Oct;57:1-29. doi: 10.1016/j.neubiorev.2015.08.003. Review.

Stroop, J. R. (1935). "Studies of interference in serial verbal reactions. Journal of experimental psychology," 18(6), 643.

Tang YY, Lu Q, Feng H, Tang R, Posner MI. (2015) "Short-term meditation increases blood flow in anterior cingulate cortex and insula." Front Psychol. 2015 Feb

26;6:212. doi: 10.3389/fpsyg.2015.00212. PMID: 25767459

Thomas J, Thomas CJ, Radcliffe J, Itsiopoulos C; (2015) "Omega-3 Fatty Acids in Early Prevention of Inflammatory Neurodegenerative Disease: A Focus on Alzheimer's Disease"; Biomed Res Int. 2015;2015:172801. doi: 10.1155/2015/172801. Epub 2015 Aug 2

Tomasino, Chiesa, Fabbro. (2014) "Disentangling the neural mechanisms involved in Hinduism- and Buddhism-related meditations"; Brain Cogn. 2014 Oct;90:32-40. doi: 10.1016/j.bandc.2014.03.013. Epub 2014 Jun 27.

Troels W. Kjaera, Camilla Bertelsena, Paola Piccinib, David Brooksb, Jørgen Alvingc, Hans C. Lou "Increased dopamine tone during meditation-induced change of consciousness"; Cognitive Brain Research 13 (2002) 255–259

Tulving, E. (1972). Episodic and semantic memory. In E. Tulving & W. Donaldson (Eds.), "Organization of Memory," (pp. 381–403). New York: Academic Press.

Tune LE; "Depression and Alzheimer's disease." Depress Anxiety. 1998;8 Suppl 1:91-5. Review.

Valkanova V, Eguia Rodriguez R, Ebmeier KP (2014) "Mind over matter: what do we know about neuroplasticity in adults?" Int Psychogeriatr. 2014 Jun;26(6):891-909. Epub 2014 Jan 2.

Velden AM, Piet J, Møller AB, Fjorback L. (2017) "Mindfulness-based cognitive therapy is efficient in the treatment of recurrent depression." Ugeskr Laeger. 2017 Jan 23;179(4). pii: V04160291. Danish. PMID: 28115049

Vestergaard-Poulsen P, van Beek M, Skewes J, Bjarkam CR, Stubberup M, Bertelsen J, Roepstorff A (2009) "Long-term meditation is associated with increased gray matter density in the brain stem." Neuroreport. 2009 Jan 28;20(2):170-4. doi: 10.1097/WNR.0b013e328320012a.

Wang DJ1, Rao H, Korczykowski M, Wintering N, Pluta J, Khalsa DS, Newberg AB.(2011); "Cerebral blood flow changes associated with different meditation practices and perceived depth of meditation"; Psychiatry Res. 2011 Jan 30;191(1):60-7. doi: 10.1016/j.pscychresns.2010.09.011. Epub 2010 Dec 8.

Yang CC, Barrós-Loscertales A, Pinazo D, Ventura-Campos N, Borchardt V, Bustamante JC, Rodríguez-Pujadas A, Fuentes-Claramonte P, Balaguer R, Ávila C, Walter M.; (2016) "State and Training Effects of Mindfulness Meditation on Brain Networks Reflect Neuronal Mechanisms of Its Antidepressant Effect"; Neural Plast. 2016;2016:9504642. doi: 10.1155/2016/9504642.PMID: 26998365

Zeidan F, Martucci KT, Kraft RA2, McHaffie JG, Coghill RC. (2013) "Neural correlates of mindfulness meditation-related anxiety relief"; Soc Cogn Affect Neurosci. 2014 Jun; 9(6):751-9. doi: 10.1093/scan/nst041. Epub 2013 Apr 24.

BIBLIOGRAPHY

Dreaming the Soul Back Home: Shamanic Dreaming for Healing and Becoming Whole Paperback – May 29, 2012; by Robert Moss

The Seat of the Soul: 25th Anniversary Edition with a Study Guide Paperback – Deluxe Edition, March 11, 2014; by Gary Zukav

The Seven Spiritual Laws of Success: A Practical Guide to the Fulfillment of Your Dreams by Deepak Chopra

You Can Heal Your Life: Paperback – January 1, 1984; by Louise Hay

Journey of Souls: Case Studies of Life Between Lives – July, 1994; by Michael Newton November 9, 1994; by Deepak Chopra

The Mind Gym: Wake Up Your Mind Paperback – January 6, 2005; by Mind Gym

Living Beautifully: with Uncertainty and Change - Oct 8, 2013; by Pema Chodron

Destiny of Souls: New Case Studies of Life Between Lives– May 8, 2000; by Michael Newton

Music

"Each Tear" by Mary J Blige –from the 2009 album *Stronger with Each Tear*

"How Awesome Is Our God" (feat. Yolanda Adams); Israel and New Breed – 2015

"Optimistic" by The by Sounds of Blackness—from the 2001 album *The Very Best of Sounds of Blackness*

"Rise Up" by Andra Day–from the 2015 album *Cheers to the Fall*